Cookie Molds Around the Year
An Almanac of Molds, Cookies, and Other Treats
— Anne L. Watson —

In this companion to *Baking with Cookie Molds*, Anne L. Watson presents cookies and molds for many holidays and all seasons, as well as for special interests and occasions—weddings, kids, story-telling around the fireplace, and much more. With nearly 150 photos of molds, cookies, and processes, *Cookie Molds Around the Year* features new techniques and new recipes, along with a month-by-month diary of the seasons on San Juan Island, Anne's home.

Author Online!

For updates, more resources, and
personal answers to your questions, visit
Anne's Cookies and Cookie Molds Page at

www.annelwatson.com/cookiemolds

Spring

Summer

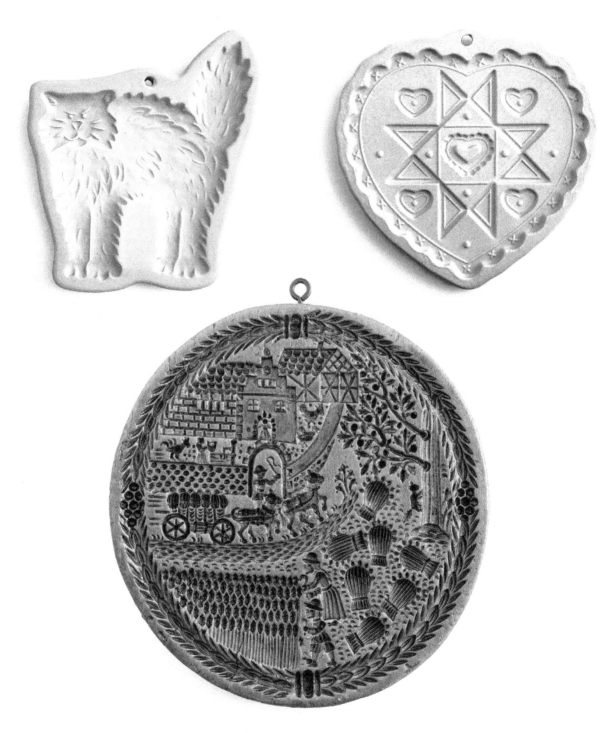

Autumn

Winter

Books by Anne L. Watson

Cookbooks
Baking with Cookie Molds
Cookie Molds Around the Year

Home Crafts
Smart Soapmaking
Milk Soapmaking
Smart Lotionmaking
Castile Soapmaking
Cool Soapmaking

Lifestyle
Smart Housekeeping
Smart Housekeeping Around the Year
Living Apart Together

Novels
Skeeter: A Cat Tale
Pacific Avenue
Joy
Flight
Cassie's Castaways
Willow's Crystal
Benecia's Mirror
A Chambered Nautilus
Departure

Cookie Molds

AROUND THE YEAR

An Almanac of Molds, Cookies, and Other Treats for Christmas, New Year's, Valentine's Day, Easter, Halloween, Thanksgiving, Other Holidays, and Every Season

Anne L. Watson

Next River Books
Bellingham, Washington

Published first as an ebook in 2016.

This book is set in Minion Pro and Presidio.

Library of Congress subject headings: Cookie molds; Cookies; Christmas cookery; Holiday cookery; Cookery, European—History; Cookery, Medieval; Cookery, German; Cookery, Dutch; Cookery, Scottish; Gingerbread; Shortbread; Cookery (Honey); Molds (Cookware)

Version 1.1

Cover: Seasons of the Heart—cookie mold by Pampered Chef

Contents

BEFORE WE BEGIN

Basic Directions for Molded Cookies

For the recipes in this book, you'll need a general knowledge of how to work with cookie molds. You'll find very detailed, illustrated instructions in my earlier book *Baking with Cookie Molds*. Here's a summary:

Using cookie molds is made much easier with my recipes, because they rely on the traditional sweetener for molded cookies, honey, rather than sugar. I've found that up to 50% of the sweetener can be sugar without creating a fragile, difficult dough, and many people do like the extra sweetness of sugar. So my recipes mostly reflect that compromise.

Using my recipes or honey-sweetened recipes of your own, you may find cookie molding to be problem-free. But if you do have difficulties, the thing I want to emphasize most is that you can solve most of them if you experiment with the mold—maybe, if it's a particularly tough one, with each kind of dough you use. Once you work out a good procedure, molding cookies is easy. But don't be discouraged if you have to try a few things before you reach that "easy" point.

Some molds do best if they're oiled lightly. Some will release easier if you use only a light coating of flour. Some work better with both oil and flour, but be careful not to use too much of either, or it will make a paste. I had one mold that drove me crazy until I tried nonstick cooking spray, which had never worked for me with any other mold.

Some molds work best if you turn them face up and roll a blob of dough into them. In other cases, you'll get your best results by rolling the dough out and pushing the mold into it face down.

Some doughs are easier to unmold than others. The easiest for me were recipes containing sieved jam, especially if the jam contained citric acid and pectin. Cookies sweetened only with honey were easier to unmold than sugar sweetened cookies. My usual mixture of half honey (or other liquid sweetener) and half sugar works well for most molds. I use 100% honey for very large or very difficult ones.

If you use margarine instead of butter, you might need to experiment to find a brand that works well with molded cookies. At one time, they all seemed to. Then, new regulations about trans fats resulted in reformulation of most margarines. I tried a number of brands with unsatisfactory results. But lately, the brands I've tested seem to work better.

For a while, I used refined coconut oil in preference to margarine, and it worked very well. But if you try that, don't let any go down your drain, or it will congeal and clog your pipes severely!

If your ingredients are giving you sticky dough that doesn't unmold well, try different options for unmolding the cookies. If unmolding from one point or direction isn't working, try another. Inward-pointing angles tend to tear, so if you can avoid unmolding a cookie that has them in a way that puts tension on that area, you'll be ahead. A sharply pointed star shaped cookie would be difficult no matter which direction you use, but for most, you can avoid problems.

Molds designed for multiple cookies are much easier to work with if you make the cookies singly.

I always use baking parchment to minimize handling the dough itself. This isn't difficult with most molds, but some are a little trickier. If you're using the mold face down like a cookie cutter, you roll the dough onto parchment. If you're using it face up, you put a piece of parchment over the surface of the dough before you roll it into the mold. Nonstick foil will work just as well.

There are more tips on preparing cookie molds in the February section of this book. And here are a couple of examples of unmolding cookies with special challenges.

Saint Nicholas

This mold, from Gene Wilson of HOBI Cookie Molds, is beautiful, but it has one big problem—the weakness of the staff that projects above the figure's shoulder. Here's how I make this cookie:

1. Flour the mold lightly.

2. Break off a blob of dough and shape it into a cylinder about the length of the mold.

3. Flour the dough cylinder lightly.

4. Press the dough into the mold, smoothing it out to cover the entire carved area. If there's not enough, I add more floured dough.

5. Cover the dough with a square of parchment.

6. Roll the parchment with a rolling pin.

7. Turn the mold over and grasp the edge of the parchment at the bottom of the figure. With this mold, it matters a lot where you start. The staff will rip if you start at the top.

8. If the dough sticks to the parchment, you're home free. Separate the cookie from the mold a little at a time, with a motion like opening a book.

9. If the dough sticks to the mold, try to tease a little of it out at the base of the figure, still holding the mold upside down. It will probably distort a little, but you can push it back into shape once the cookie is unmolded.

10. Once you get it started, it is going to come out of the mold if you're patient and gentle. The force of gravity is on your side—a formidable ally.

Large Nativity

My large nativity mold from House on the Hill is a foot in diameter, and it's not difficult to get *something*, but it's not easy to get a clear all-over print. Here's the cookie you make from it:

The border is difficult to print consistently, and I made many tries where one or another of the figures was blurry.

After a few efforts with uneven results, I marked the back of the mold with a black permanent marker to indicate where harder pressure was needed. I also realized that the entire border needed special treatment.

The mold is composition, which releases easier than most materials, so light flouring was adequate to ensure that the dough wouldn't stick.

These instructions describe how I finally got consistent results:

1. With the lightly floured mold face up, press lightly floured dough into the mold to cover it fairly smoothly.

2. Lay a sheet of parchment over the mold to cover it completely. Roll with rolling pin. Break off any awkward excess, but keep a small margin to be trimmed off later.

3. Cover the parchment with a stiff flat surface like a cutting board. Flip the cookie so that the dough is on the bottom, mold on top. Slide the cutting board out so that the sandwich of parchment/dough/mold is flat on your counter or table.

4. Press hard on the margin and on the other marked spots. Or even pound it lightly with the side of your fist.

5. Using the parchment and the margin as "grabbers," *very* gradually and gently unmold the cookie as described above for St. Nicholas.

How to Tell When Cookies Are Done

Cookies are done when they're brown, right?

Well, no. By the time cookies look brown, they're overdone.

For one thing, just like a roast or a casserole, cookies don't stop cooking suddenly when you take them out of the oven. So don't wait until you're sure they're done to take them out. If they really are underbaked when they're cool, it won't hurt anything if you put them back in the oven and bake them a little more.

Keep in mind that an oven light, if you have one, doesn't give you the best color rendition. Mine always makes the cookies look paler than they really are. If I trust it, I end up with overbaked cookies.

Cookies are usually done when they've just started to brown at the edges. Given the lighting problem with ovens, you may have to remove the sheet and look at it in natural light to get a good view of this.

But the big thing is how the bottom of the cookie looks. If it is slightly brown, with no doughy-looking spots, the cookie is done, regardless of the color. So I take my cookie sheet out of the oven, put on a heat glove (or use a spatula), flip a cookie over, and check the bottom.

And sometimes, depending on airflow in your oven, part of a sheet of cookies will be ready while the rest need more time. If that happens, there's no problem with taking the cookie sheet out of the oven, removing the fully baked cookies, and returning the underdone ones to the oven.

I usually put the cookies on a cooling rack right away. Occasionally, I have a very large cookie that seems not quite done in the middle, but is getting too brown at the edge. I'll leave it on the cookie sheet for a few minutes to let the stored heat in the metal help it finish cooking.

Two-layer baking sheets with air in the middle will keep cookies from actually burning, but they still overbake. Since these sheets can't be washed in the dishwasher, I'm not a fan.

One thing to remember is an old saying: "If you can smell it in here, it's burning in there." Use a timer.

Shaping Cookie Tartlets

There are many recipes for small cookie tartlets in this book. Here's how I shape them, using a tart mold such as this one from Brown Cookie.

This is really just an extra-easy way of doing something that was simple to begin with. The basic idea is to roll a sheet of dough, remove a small strip to create two or more rows, and then press with the mold, cut, and trim off the scraps. This saves handling and re-rolling, both of which toughen your dough.

1. In the photo to the left, I've rolled and trimmed a sheet of dough for cookie tartlets. (If you want to be super accurate, you can use rolling pin guides to make the rolled sheet perfectly flat and uniform).

Notice that I've rolled it on a sheet of nonstick foil. This is important, because it makes it possible to cut and bake the cookies without handling any of them.

2. When you have your sheet rolled and trimmed, set your mold on it and decide how many lines of cookies you can make. Then cut a channel to separate the lines.

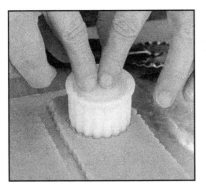

3. Now press and cut your cookies. If you're using tart molds, assemble the mold and place it on the dough. Press down on the center piece, then on the outer cutter. Then lift the cutter off the dough—remove the center piece first, then the outer cutter. Press the center piece down lightly with your forefinger to help separate them.

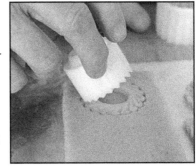

4. Tip the center piece to remove it without lifting the cookie from the foil.

5. Now cut the dough, remove the scraps, and continue to the next cookie.

6. Here's my sheet with three cookies cut out. I'll keep shaping and cutting them until all the dough has been used. Note that I haven't touched the cookies themselves, just removed the scraps around them.

7. Transfer the aluminum foil sheet to a baking sheet for baking.

Other small molds and cookie stamps would be used in a similar way, but instead of working with the built-in cutter piece, you'd use a cookie cutter after you'd pressed the image with the mold.

JANUARY

New Year's, Twelfth Night, and Storytelling around the Fireplace

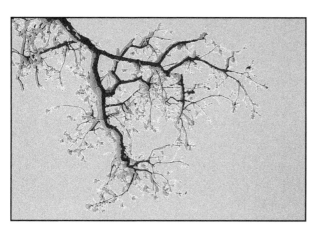

For most of the years I've lived in the Pacific Northwest, December has been the coldest, stormiest month. I try to regard January as the beginning of the path to spring. But it can be very cold, and the days are still short. At the 49th Parallel, darkness comes early on a January evening.

The month begins with the New Year's revels, celebrating new beginnings and good intentions. Next comes Feast of the Three Kings on January 6. This is Twelfth Night, the "twelfth day of Christmas," and a now little-observed tradition is that Christmas decorations should be removed on that day, and not before.

After that, the holidays are over, the Christmas lights no longer sparkle. But we have a new light—or an old one, for it goes back farther than history—storytelling around the fire. Or, in our case, the fireplace.

And stories are a form of light in themselves, because they call on the light of the imagination. They truly enlighten us—tell us who we are, and who we can be. Stories are one of the great powers in human history. The power of stories may be the source of the belief in magic.

No time is more magical than the gathering of faces around the fireplace, and the first words of a story that binds them together. So join me for an evening of stories and cookies.

Recipe: Lemon Shortbread Cookie Tartlets

Serve with champagne and strawberries.

    1 cup (225 grams) unsalted butter , softened
    ½ cup (100 grams) sugar
    1 tablespoon honey
    1 teaspoon freshly squeezed lemon juice
    1 teaspoon finely grated lemon peel
    ⅛ teaspoon culinary lemon oil
    About 2½ cups (350 grams) all-purpose flour
        (plain flour)
    Lemon curd
    Strawberries

1. Cream the butter, sugar, and honey.

2. Combine the lemon juice, lemon peel, and lemon oil and add to the butter mixture.

3. Add all-purpose flour (plain flour) slowly until the mixture is solid enough to knead.

4. Transfer to your work surface and knead in all but the last ¼ cup (35 grams) of all-purpose flour (plain flour).

5. Add up to the remaining ¼ cup (35 grams) of all-purpose flour (plain flour) slowly and carefully, checking the texture of your dough as you go. Stop adding when the dough still feels slightly tacky but no longer sticks to your work surface.

6. When the flour amount seems right, wrap and set aside. Do not chill before molding.

7. Detailed, illustrated directions for using cookie tart molds are located at the beginning of this book. I recommend molding and baking a test cookie to make sure your dough is correct. If you haven't added enough flour, the cookies won't hold an impression.

8. Preheat the oven to 300°F (150°C).

9. Bake the test cookie for 10 to 15 minutes or until the edges have slightly browned and the top has begun to firm up.

10. Examine the test cookie. If it has spread during baking and the design has become blurry, knead a little more flour into the rest of the dough and repeat the test.

11. When you have good results from the test, form and bake the rest of the cookies as instructed above.

12. Cool the cookies and spread the center of each thinly with lemon curd. Serve the berries alongside the cookies or top each cookie tart with a thin slice of strawberry.

First Story: Journey to the Twelfth-Night Market

In a town not far from you, there lived a farmer who was a miserable man. His farm was prosperous, but his wife was bitter and his children were frightened, for he cared only for his farm and the wealth that came from it, and he was never kind to them at all.

He blamed them for their sorrow, for he believed that anyone could be happy if only they would. "They are whining fools," he thought. "The wife and children of a poor man might have something to cry about. Mine live in comfort, but they cry anyway."

"Smile!" he commanded his children. So they stretched their mouths, but they could not really smile, and he turned away in disappointment.

"Sing!" he commanded his wife. "Why do other men's wives sing as they go about their work, but you do not?"

So his wife tried to sing, but her voice broke with tears, and he turned away in disgust.

Now, it came time for the Feast of Twelfth Night, and the farmer took his wares to market, for it was the best market of the year. Surely, if he brought home a bag of gold, his wife and children would smile and sing.

"They would be fools if they didn't," he thought grimly.

So he set out with a goose he had killed, a basket of fresh-caught fish, and a suckling pig that had been only that morning with its mother.

The way to the market was dangerous, for many robbers lay in wait to catch a farmer with his wares on the way there, or with his bag of gold on the way home. And a dark, fast-flowing river ran between his farm and the market, and the fording of that river was a treacherous thing.

When he was halfway there, the goose struggled in his hand, and tears poured from its eyes.

"Let me go," it said. "I never intended to give my life for a stranger's dinner!"

The man was astonished, but he did not let go of the goose.

"A goose that can talk and cry will bring a fine price at the market," said the farmer. "I would be a fool to let you go."

"Let me go, and I will grant the wish of your heart," the goose said.

The farmer was suspicious. "How can a goose know the wish of my heart, let alone grant it?"

"How indeed, if you do not know it yourself? But for a goose who can come back to life after you have wrung its neck, granting the wish of your heart is a small thing," said the goose.

So the farmer let the goose go, and it flew off into the sky. "Of course I know the wish of my heart," he thought. "I wish to escape the robbers as I journey to the market." He walked on with a lighter heart, and he thought it was because he had no more need to fear the robbers.

Soon he came to the river. As he stood on the bank, his fish began to writhe in their basket, and tears poured from their eyes.

"Let us go!" they cried. "For we never intended to give our lives for a stranger's dinner!"

The farmer was bewildered, but he did not put them into the river.

"Fish that can talk and cry will bring many bags of gold at the market," he said. "I let the goose go, but I would be a fool to let you go."

"If you let us go, we will grant the wish of your heart," said the fish. "That is nothing, to fish that can drown in the air and still come back to life."

The farmer considered their offer. If the goose had granted him safety from the robbers, surely the fish could bring him safe across the river. And the piglet would fetch a good price at the market, enough that his wife and children would have to smile and sing.

So he let the fish go, and they swam along the current. "Now I can cross the river and sell my piglet at the market," the farmer said.

He put the piglet on his head and crossed the water easily. He walked on with a lighter heart, and he thought it was because he had no more need to fear the river.

But as he came to the market, the piglet began to squirm, and tears poured from its eyes.

"Take me home to my mother," it pleaded. "I never intended to give my life for a stranger's dinner. Take me home, and I will grant the wish of your heart."

"I would be a fool to go home with empty hands," said the farmer. "And I have no more fear of the robbers or the river, so you have nothing to offer me."

"You have a hidden wish," said the piglet. "And for a talking pig, granting a wish, even a hidden wish, is no great thing."

The farmer considered this third offer.

"What is this wish?" he asked.

"Your hidden wish is to find what you have lost—the heart of the boy you used to be. When you released the goose and the fish, you thought your heart was lighter because you were safe from the robbers and the river.

"But you were wrong. Your heart was lighter because you showed mercy to the goose and the fish, and did not count their lives as money in your pocket. That was the wish they granted you, to regain part of yourself.

"Take me home to my mother, show mercy to me, and reclaim the rest of your heart. That is the gift you will bring your wife and children from the great market of Twelfth Night."

So the farmer turned, and the piglet followed him home. The farmer's children smiled and danced to see their father so changed, and his wife sang and laughed.

And the piglet returned to its mother and never spoke another word.

Anne L. Watson

Recipe: Spiced Lemon Pecan "King" Cookies

These cookies are based on "King Cake," the traditional Twelfth Night dessert in New Orleans, where I grew up. Traditionally, a bean, coin, or favor is placed in the cake , and the person whose piece of cake includes the favor must host the king cake party the next year.

1 cup (225 grams) unsalted butter
1 large egg
½ cup (120 milliliters) honey

1 tablespoon freshly squeezed lemon juice
1 teaspoon natural lemon flavoring
½ cup (100 grams) sugar
2 teaspoons finely grated lemon peel
1 teaspoon cinnamon
½ teaspoon nutmeg
⅛ teaspoon salt
½ cup (80 grams) chopped pecans
About 4½ cups (630 grams) all-purpose flour
    (plain flour)

1. Preheat the oven to 350°F (175°C), or lower for especially thick cookies.

2. Grind the pecans and one cup of the flour together in a food processor with the steel blade. Set aside.

3. Melt the butter and set aside.

4. Beat the egg in a large bowl until the yolk and white are fully mixed.

5. Mix the honey, lemon juice, and lemon flavoring. Add to the egg and beat until well mixed.

6. Mix the sugar, grated lemon peel, cinnamon, nutmeg, and salt. Add to the egg mixture and beat until well mixed.

7. Add the melted butter slowly and beat until well mixed. Don't just pour it in quickly—the heat still in the butter could cook the egg!

8. Add the flour/pecan mixture.

9. Transfer the dough to a floured work surface. Continue adding flour by kneading in a little at a time until the dough is smooth and slightly sticky.

10. Wrap or cover the dough to prevent drying as you work.

11. Roll and form the dough.

11. Bake for 10 to 15 minutes or until the edges have slightly browned and the top has begun to firm up.

Second Story: The Ropedancer

In a town not far from you, there lived a widow who fretted greatly about her only son. He was a handsome boy, with golden hair and a bright smile, and he was a good boy, too. He meant to be no trouble to his mother, but the two of them might have been from different countries, so unlike were they.

The widow owned a fine bakeshop that she had from her late husband, and she counted on her son to follow in his father's path, learn to make bread and pastries, and take care of her in her old age.

Since his mother had no other children, the boy understood that her future was in his hands, but it was a great trouble to him. For he had little skill at baking and little interest in learning the trade. And, try as he might, he could hardly conceal his feelings.

She tried to graft her skill into his hands, her love of good baking into his mind. But bread knows when a baker does not care about it. There was nothing really wrong with his loaves, but there was nothing very right with them either. They were discouraged loaves, and they discouraged those who ate them instead of making them stronger.

She thought he might marry a girl with a better hand for baking, and for a long time she hoped he would turn his eye to the neighbor's daughter, a fine young girl who often helped in the bakery. She had the hand for bread, and for pastry too, and the widow knew her shop would thrive beyond the next generation if her son married the neighbor's daughter.

But one year her son came home from the fair with a light in his eyes, and stories about a man who juggled and danced on a rope. And her heart sank, for this was no profession for a widow's only son. She said nothing as his baking became worse than before, and she held her tongue when she saw a rope stretched between two trees in the wood behind their house. When he limped into the bakeshop with his ankle bound up one morning, she hoped pain had taught him a lesson about rope dancing. But she could see in his face that, however little his body might be able to follow them, his dreams were dancing and spinning on a rope high above a crowd.

She sighed, for she knew about dreams. Her father had opposed her marriage because her chosen husband was a baker, a tradesman, not a landowner. She knew that arguing with someone else's dream was as fruitless as arguing with one's own. She hoped her son would forget dancing and juggling if she said nothing. The acrobats were gone, and she hoped they would never come back. He would surely forget.

He might have, for he had no teacher. But one day, as he stood outside the bakery with the neighbor's daughter, a songbird came near them, pecking the ground for crumbs. And the girl flapped her apron at the bird to shoo it away.

"Why do you do that?" the boy asked, laying a hand on her arm to stop her.

"The birds are dirty," she said. "The come for the crumbs, but they quarrel and soil the path, and I do not like them here."

"Surely, everyone must eat," he said. "But if you prefer, we will put a feeder in the back garden. For we have crumbs enough for a thousand birds, and where else should they go?"

The girl was surprised, but she agreed that birds in the back garden would not be a bad thing. So he built a feeder for them and kept it filled with crumbs.

When he next struggled with his ropewalking, he noticed a bird sitting on a branch near him. After he had fallen once or twice, the bird spoke up:

"Bend your legs a little," it said. "Keep the rope at the center of your foot, and look out, not down."

The boy had never heard a bird talk, but after a moment of surprise, he realized that a bird would know far more about walking on a line than any man. So he took the bird's advice, and soon he could walk easily on the rope.

He had little time, though, and it galled him to have to leave the bird and return to his endless baking. But when he next came to practice, he found another bird, and another, and among them, they taught him to walk on the line, and to turn and dance as well, so that he lacked nothing in skill. And he saw he could go and make his fortune with the juggler folk, and that he had no more reason to be a baker, save one.

That was his mother, and he knew he must leave her in peace and safety or he could not leave at all. So he begged the neighbor girl to be a daughter to her, and to learn all the business of the shop, and never leave.

"Your talent is greater than mine," he said. "And my mother needs you."

"I will do it," she promised. "For no one else does need me. And your mother has been like a mother to me.

"And besides," she added, "I love making the loaves, and the sweets, with the fine smell of wheat and spices. Being the daughter of the bakeshop is my dream come to waking."

Then the boy told his mother what he planned to do. At first she wept, but soon she realized that her new daughter was a much better heir for her business than ever her son could be.

"You must come back sometimes," she said. "You must let us see you, and hear of your life, or we will fret about you night and day."

He promised to do this whenever he could. And he also asked the girl to keep the feeder full for the birds, winter and summer, for it made him sad to think they might go hungry. And this she promised. So he left to seek his fortune with the jugglers.

Now, whether he became a famous ropedancer, the story does not say. Nor whether he traveled to many lands, or if he performed for kings and queens. It may well be, for all who saw him marveled that he danced so like a bird, it seemed he might well fly.

But it is known that he kept his promise to come back from time to time, and that he did all he could for his mother for as long as she lived. The neighbor's daughter welcomed him when he came as she welcomed the birds to the well-filled feeder behind the house. And, when the time came for him to go, the girl showed no more surprise or reproach than when the birds flew away.

There are those who believe he returned to stay, in the end. For in later years, an old man could be seen, teaching a golden-haired child to walk on a rope in the woods behind the house, while the neighbor's daughter, now an old woman, kneaded her wonderful bread in the kitchen behind the bakeshop. But whether it was the ropedancer at all, or whether the child was his, no one would ever know.

Anne L. Watson

Tip: Matching Cookies and Molds

When you make molded cookies, it's important to think about the match between your recipe and the mold you want to use.

Cookie recipes make dough that varies in color, texture, and "pattern"—that is, whether it has speckles of color. It also varies in how tender the cookie is after it's cooked.

Making sure you have a good match between the cookie and the mold is one of many reasons why it's a good idea to bake a test cookie.

Color

The things that add color to dough are fairly obvious—chocolate, cocoa, coffee, spices, etc. Almost all are strong flavors, and you want them for that. But, if you use them in your dough, you have to choose a cookie mold that isn't too small or delicate in pattern. A larger, more deeply cut cookie mold will give you a prettier cookie with a dark dough. One thing to realize, though, is that the dough is going to be darker than the baked cookie, because quite a bit of liquid bakes out of the cookie.

Texture

Some ingredients like chocolate chips, chopped nuts, dried fruit, or oatmeal just don't marry well with cookie molds. You need a smooth, dense surface to print the pattern of a mold. If you want these ingredients, you can make layer cookies. Or you can make sandwich cookies or cookie tartlets, with the special ingredients in the filling. Or you can grind nuts and replace part of the flour with them. If you use dried fruit, even in layer cookies, it must be chopped much finer than you'd expect, because it will rehydrate and enlarge once it gets into the dough. Of course, you might rehydrate it with brandy or other flavoring *before* you put it into the dough, then chop it. I haven't tried this, but it would probably work, with a little experimentation.

Pattern

Some ingredients like maple sugar or spices may make speckles in the dough. This works fine with some molds, not with others. A flower design with dark speckles is likely to look as if it has Black Spot. Faces might look strange. But geometric patterns or animals won't seem odd with speckles. This is also a matter of scale—a large speckled figure might look fine, while a close-up of a face might not.

Tenderness

The more tender a cookie is, the smaller it must be to hold together. Tenderness is affected by the kind of flour you use— softer flours such as cake flour, pastry flour, or Southern US all-purpose flour, will make tenderer cookies. Butter and sugar proportions also affect tenderness. So does use of honey—when I make enormous cookies, I use 100% honey rather than half sugar and half honey. They're harder and denser than all-sugar cookies.

Handling also affects tenderness. The more you knead dough, the tougher it will be.

I always make shortbread with soft flour, and I use tiny molds. For most other cookies, there's a wider range. Most molds can tolerate a variety of color, texture, and pattern.

I wouldn't use extra soft flour for any cookie over an inch or so in any dimension. For those over eight inches, I'd use 100% honey. I'm not saying it couldn't work to break those rules, but I like to make things easy on myself.

Tip: Layer Cookies

Layering dough creates an opportunity to add ingredients that don't mold well. The basic idea is to create a laminated sheet of rolled dough with plain dough on the top—the side that contacts the cookie mold—and dough with tasty tidbits such as dried cranberries or miniature chocolate chips in the bottom layer.

It's a great idea for adding variety to molded cookies, but it has one tricky moment and one real disadvantage, which I'll explain as we go along.

Here's how to make layer cookies for molding:

1. Divide the dough into two balls, one about twice the size of the other.

2. Set the smaller ball of dough aside.

3. Knead tasty tidbits such as chopped fruit or nuts or miniature chocolate chips into the larger ball of dough.

4. Roll out each ball or dough separately on sheets of nonstick aluminum foil. Make them into fairly even rectangles, about equal in width and length. This means the rolled-out dough from the larger ball of dough will be about twice as thick as the rolled out dough from the smaller ball.

5. Fair warning—this is the tricky step. Slip a sheet of something fairly solid under each sheet of foil. I use two of those almost-paper-thin plastic cutting mats, but you could use cardboard, flat cookie sheets, or almost any other rigid or semi-rigid thin, flat object. When you have a secure backing of this kind beneath each sheet of rolled-out dough, line them up and press them together, rather like closing a book. They won't line up perfectly, but you can improve them a little in the next steps.

6. Set aside the cutting mats, or whatever you used as solid sheets in step 5. You're through with them. Now you have a

"sandwich" consisting of a layer of foil, a layer of cookie dough with tidbits, a plain cookie dough layer, and another layer of foil on top. Remove the foil from the plain cookie dough layer and lay the dough down on the counter.

7. Lightly roll the two layers together. This is your chance to piece and straighten a little at the edges to get a double layer in places where the match wasn't perfect. Trim the edges.

8. Now you have a layered sheet of dough. The disadvantage of this technique is that you only have one chance to mold it. You can't re-roll scraps without losing the layering. So either cut it carefully into pieces about the size of your molds, or use a springerle rolling pin. In any case, minimize the scraps.

(Of course you can still make cookies from the scraps, and they'll be good, but they're not layer cookies. I don't even try to mold my layering scraps, just cut them with a cookie cutter. No one has refused to eat them yet.)

9. Mold and bake the cookies just as you would any other dough.

All-Over Pattern Rolling Pin

When you're making layer cookies, you can't re-roll the dough and keep the layers. So you want to get as many cookies as possible out of the first rolling. My favorite cookie mold for this is a springerle rolling pin with an all-over pattern. Mine is antique, but they are still made. Besides working so well for layer cookies, these are great for making a lot of molded cookies quickly.

When you've rolled your dough, and stacked the two layers, you flour the top lightly, make an all-over design on it with one of these rolling pins, and then cut it into cookies, either with shaped cookie cutters (I use a fluted rectangle) or with a pastry wheel.

Recipe: Raisin Layer Cookies

The cookie is mild flavored, somewhat similar to a Garibaldi. The raisins are in the lower layer. If you want a stronger flavor, increase the spices and flavorings and add finely grated orange rind to the lower layer along with the raisins.

    1 cup (225 grams) unsalted butter
    1 large egg
    ½ cup (120 milliliters) honey
    1 tablespoon cream
    1 teaspoon natural lemon flavoring
    ½ teaspoon natural orange flavoring

¼ teaspoon almond extract

½ cup (100 grams) sugar

½ cup (80 grams) ground blanched almonds (See note.)

½ teaspoon ground ginger (or 2 teaspoons grated fresh
    ginger)

¼ teaspoon ground cloves

½ teaspoon ground cinnamon

¼ teaspoon salt

½ cup (75 grams) chopped raisins

About 3¾ cups (515 grams) all-purpose flour (plain
    flour)

1. Melt the butter and set aside.

2. Beat the egg in a large bowl until yolk and white are fully mixed.

3. Mix the honey, cream, lemon flavoring, orange flavoring, and almond extract. Add to the egg and beat until well mixed. If you're using fresh ginger, add it to this mixture.

4. Mix the sugar, ground almonds, ground ginger, cloves, cinnamon, and salt. Add to the egg mixture and beat until well mixed.

5. Add the melted butter slowly and beat until well mixed.

6. Add flour slowly until the mixture is solid enough to knead.

7. Transfer to your work surface and knead in more flour to make a soft, slightly sticky dough.

8. Form cookies according to directions for layer cookies in the preceding article.

9. Refrigerate the cookies while you preheat the oven to 350°F (175°C), or lower for especially thick cookies.

10. Bake for 10 to 15 minutes or until the edges have slightly browned and the top has begun to firm up, longer for extra-large cookies.

Notes

Blanched almonds are almonds with the brown skins removed. It's not necessary to blanch them, but your cookies will be quite speckled if you don't. You may be able to find almonds already ground, or you can mix whole almonds with one cup of the flour and process in a food processor with a steel blade. The flour keeps the almonds from turning into almond butter in the processor. If you grind the almonds with part of the flour, add them right after you add the butter, and before the rest of the flour.

To chop raisins, sprinkle a little flour on them. This will keep them from sticking to your knife. I've tried chopping them in a food processor, but even with the sprinkled flour, a knife does a better job.

Recipe: Spice Cookies

The flavor is somewhere between snickerdoodles and graham crackers. Because of the graham flour, this dough is more inclined to stick to molds than most. Flour the rolled out dough more heavily than most, and see the tip in the article following this recipe for removing any stray bits of flour from molded dough.

1 cup (225 grams) unsalted butter
1 large egg
½ cup (120 milliliters) honey
1 tablespoon cream
1 teaspoon brandy flavoring
½ cup (100 grams) dark brown sugar
½ teaspoon ground cinnamon
½ teaspoon ground mace
¼ teaspoon ground cloves
⅛ teaspoon ground cardamom
¼ teaspoon salt
1 cup (120 grams) graham flour or whole wheat flour
About 4½ cups (630 grams) all-purpose flour (plain flour)

1. Melt the butter and set aside.

2. Beat the egg in a large bowl until yolk and white are fully mixed.

3. Mix the honey, cream, and brandy flavoring. Add to the egg and beat until well mixed.

4. Mix the brown sugar, cinnamon, cloves, mace, cardamom and salt. Add to the egg mixture and beat until well mixed.

5. Add the melted butter slowly and beat until well mixed.

6. Add graham flour slowly, then add all-purpose flour (plain flour) until the mixture is solid enough to knead.

7. Transfer to your work surface and knead in more all-purpose flour (plain flour) to make a soft, slightly sticky dough.

9. Roll and form the dough.

10. Chill the cookies while you preheat the oven to 350°F (177°C).

11. Bake for 10 to 15 minutes or until slightly browned at the edges.

Tip: Removing Extra Flour

Some doughs just want to stick to your molds. One way to get around this is to brush flour fairly heavily on the dough surface before molding. "Fairly" heavily doesn't mean you have a whole layer of flour, but that you can see it clearly—it isn't just a whitish veil.

But if you do use extra flour, what's likely to happen is that you'll unmold the cookie and find that it's perfect except that there are some white spots on it. Don't panic.

The first thing to do is just set the cookie aside for about fifteen minutes at room temperature. Some or all of the flour is going to disappear. If any is left, you can remove it with a lightly oiled artist's brush, either before or after baking. If there's still quite a bit, try freezing the cookie solid and then removing the flour with a lightly oiled artist's brush.

And finally, you can use that same brush to remove flecks after baking.

Of course, this is for fairly minor cleanup—a cookie that has a few spots. If you have a coating of flour all over the cookie, you may be able to remove it, possibly after chilling or freezing, with a clean pastry brush (not the same one you brush flour onto the dough with). If there's a heavy all-over coating, though, you'll probably have to mold the cookie again.

Expect a few mistakes, but with practice, this gets simple.

Third Story: The White Cat

In a town not far from you, there lived an old grazier who owned many acres and a fine flock of sheep. He was not a bad man, not at all. But he had an enemy, and this enemy lived inside his mouth. And it often spoke harsh words to his wife and his young son.

The grazier's unkind words did not come from his heart, but from whisperings of fear. His wife was a young woman, pretty and kind, and he saw no reason for her to love an old man whose best years were behind him.

As for the son, the grazier felt that sternness would raise him to stout manhood, while babying would only spoil him.

Often enough, he changed his mind, and saw his wife as the fine woman she was, and his son as a good boy with much promise. But he could not take back his hard words, for his enemy would not speak an apology. So he would take his son for an hour of playing with the lambs or buy his wife a silken ribbon for her hair.

His wife did not want hair ribbons, but she treasured them in a box at the bottom of a chest. Sometimes their soft brightness was her only reminder that her husband loved her. And this she wanted very much. So sometimes she would open the box and touch them, taking comfort from their beauty.

Now, it happened one winter morning that the grazier was sullen and his wife was slow on her feet, for they both had been up most of the night with the lambing. They had slept fitfully, the little sleep they had, and risen later than usual, and a long day was ahead of them, with more lambs yet to be born.

The grazier looked over the breakfast she had hastily and tiredly prepared.

"No proper wife would set such a meal before her husband," the enemy said. "I slept little enough last night, and have much work to do today. Surely you married me for my lands and flocks, for if you loved me, you would care about my well-being."

He felt a pang even as the words fell from his lips, for his wife had shared the lambing vigil with him without complaint, and he saw the hurt his words had added to the tiredness in her face. But she did not answer.

She went about her morning chores with a heavy heart, wondering if in fact she did still love her husband. He was like a wind that blew—now from the north, now from the south, with no way of knowing where it would shift next. And her feelings for him had a feather's balance—love and sorrow, sorrow and love, and she did not know what to do.

Fingering one of her precious ribbons in her pocket, she walked down the lane to the great road that ran to the town. She pulled her shawl close around her against the winter wind, and sat on a rock that made a natural seat beside the road.

Her thoughts stumbled and whirled. First she thought it would be best to leave the grazier forever, but she instantly changed her mind. For she did love her husband, and she knew he was not a bad man, however bitterly he might speak in his dark moods. And to abandon her child was something she could not do, but there was no way to keep the boy safe if she took him with her along the great road.

Snow lay on the verges, and at first she did not notice the white cat, even though it sat close by. When she did, she realized it was preparing to leap across the road in pursuit of something in the hedge on the other side. And at the same time, she heard a cart coming fast along the road, and she was sure the cat, intent on its leap, would be crushed by the horses' hooves and the pounding wheels.

She reached out a hand and gently held the cat as the cart passed by. It turned and looked at her with bright blue eyes, and she knew it must be deaf, for many cats with that coloring cannot hear at all.

When the cart had passed, she released it, but it did not cross the road. It regarded her for a moment with a deep, bright blue stare, meowed once, and turned back the way it had come. She watched it as it disappeared into the snowy landscape. And then she returned to her house, determined to do the best she could to bear her husband's churlishness, if only for the sake of her child.

But from that day forward, she could not hear any unkind word. Each time her husband's enemy spewed abuse, she was as deaf to it as a blue-eyed cat. What she heard instead was animal cries—the wild bleating of lambs or the shrieks of frightened chickens.

"My dear," she would say, "We must go to the sheep, for there is surely a wolf in the yard." Or "My dear, we must see to the chickens, for the wolf must be among them."

And they would rush to care for the animals, and return puzzled, for they found nothing, not even tracks in the snow near the barns.

"I saw nothing," he said one day as they returned to their house after yet another commotion.

"Nor I," she said. "Perhaps the animals heard a wolf caught in a trap."

The grazier's enemy was desperate, for without being fed by hurt, it must starve. So it tried its might against the boy, but he, too, heard only animals yammering with fear.

"Father, the wolf is here again," he cried. And the grazier rushed to defend his sheep, and again he found nothing, not even tracks in the snow near the barns.

Finally, the grazier's enemy had none to abuse but him. So, alone in the house one day, the grazier spoke his venom to himself. But all he could hear was a distant howling, and looking in a mirror, he saw a maddened wolf, snarling in a trap.

Then he took his handkerchief from his pocket, and spat his wizened enemy into it. He laid the handkerchief on the fire, and it flared and burned to an ash and less than an ash. And instantly the mirror showed him a man who was not a bad man, not at all.

That was the end of the enemy, and of the cries and uproar in the grazier's yards. His wife and son forgot his unkindness as if it had never been. And the silken ribbons were forgotten too, in their box at the bottom of the chest, for his wife had no need to look anywhere but his face for reasons to believe he loved her.

Anne L. Watson

Recipe: Chocolate Coconut Tea Cookies

The flavor is mostly like hot cocoa, with a more subtle coconut taste. For stronger chocolate flavor, make these as cookie tartlets with a chocolate filling (see notes for filling suggestions), use chocolate backing (recipe follows), or make as a layer cookie with mini chocolate chips in the lower layer. If you add a chocolate backing, you could flavor that with coconut extract as well.

Although the dough is quite dark, the finished cookies are about the color of cocoa, which means that the details of your molds won't be lost.

> ½ cup (115 grams) unsalted butter
> 1 large egg
> 1 cup (235 milliliters) canned cream of coconut (See notes.)
> 1 tablespoon coconut extract
> 1 teaspoon chocolate extract
> ½ teaspoon vanilla
> ½ cup (100 grams) sugar
> 2 tablespoons cocoa
> 1 teaspoon cinnamon
> ¼ teaspoon salt
> About 4½ cups (630 grams) all-purpose flour (plain flour)

1. Melt the butter and set aside.

2. Beat the egg in a large bowl until yolk and white are fully mixed.

3. Mix the cream of coconut, coconut extract, chocolate extract, and vanilla extract. Add to the egg and beat until well mixed.

4. Mix the sugar, cocoa, cinnamon, and salt. Add to the egg mixture and beat until well mixed.

5. Add the melted butter slowly and beat until well mixed.

6. Add flour slowly until the mixture is solid enough to knead.

7. Transfer to your work surface and knead in more flour to make a soft, slightly sticky dough.

8. Wrap or cover the dough and refrigerate for up to ½ hour—until it's firm but still flexible.

9. Roll and form the dough

10. Refrigerate the cookies while you preheat the oven to 350°F (175°C), or lower for especially thick cookies.

11. Bake for 10 to 15 minutes or until the edges have slightly browned and the top has begun to firm up.

Notes

Cream of coconut is a sweetened mixture used in drinks and desserts. It is not to be confused with coconut cream, which is unsweetened. Like natural peanut butter, cream of coconut tends to separate, so stir to blend well before measuring.

Filling suggestions for cookie tartlets: Chocolate buttercream frosting or chocolate almond butter.

Tip: Chocolate Backing

A thin (or not-so-thin) layer of chocolate on the bottom of molded cookies adds a luxurious taste to the plainer ones and takes even the tastiest to a whole new level.

The backing—unlike frosting—sets hard, so the cookies can be set on a plate with their molded sides up. You can use white chocolate, baking chocolate, or a dark chocolate (plain chocolate) like semisweet or bittersweet, or a blend of types.

> 6 ounces (170 grams) semisweet, bittersweet, or other
>   dark chocolate (plain chocolate)
> 2 tablespoons vegetable shortening (vegetable lard)
> 1½ tablespoons honey or light corn syrup
> ¾ teaspoon vanilla extract

1. While the cookies are still baking, combine the chocolate, shortening, and honey in an ovenproof container.

2. After baking the last sheet of cookies, turn off the oven and immediately put the container with the backing ingredients in the oven.

3. When the chocolate is soft and the shortening has melted, remove from the oven and stir gently to blend.

4. Add the vanilla extract and stir until well mixed.

5. When the cookies are cool, apply the chocolate mixture to their backs with an icing knife, table knife, or similar tool. Place the chocolate-backed cookies facedown on waxed paper.

6. Wait for the chocolate to set before turning upright.

Notes

Chocolate may still hold its shape when softened, so test with a spoon.

Recipe: Lime Cookies

My birthday is in January, and my favorite flavor is any fruit flavor. When I was a child, my mother worked out a lime cake for my birthday, since most other fruits weren't available in midwinter. Here's a cookie that recreates the flavor. I like it best as either a cookie tart or a sandwich cookie with lime curd filling.

1 cup (225 grams) unsalted butter
1 large egg
½ cup (120 milliliters) honey
1 tablespoon freshly squeezed lime juice
1 teaspoon freshly squeezed lemon juice

1 teaspoon natural lemon flavoring
⅛ teaspoon natural lime oil
½ cup (100 grams) sugar
2 teaspoons finely grated lime peel
1 teaspoon finely grated lemon peel
⅛ teaspoon salt
About 4½ cups (630 grams) all-purpose flour (plain
    flour)

1. Melt the butter and set aside.

2. Beat the egg in a large bowl until the yolk and white are fully mixed.

3. Mix the honey, lime juice, lemon juice, lemon flavoring, and lime oil. Add to the egg and beat until well mixed.

4. Mix the sugar, lime peel, lemon peel, and salt. Add to the egg mixture and beat until well mixed. If the mixture isn't smooth, don't worry—it will become smooth as you add the flour.

5. Add the melted butter slowly and beat until well mixed. Don't just pour it in quickly—the heat still in the butter could cook the egg!

6. Add flour slowly and mix in until you have dough that is solid enough to knead.

7. Transfer the dough to a floured work surface. Continue adding flour by kneading in a little at a time until the dough is smooth and slightly sticky.

8. Wrap or cover the dough to prevent drying, then refrigerate to make it less sticky. This should take half an hour at most.

9. Roll and form the dough.

10. Refrigerate the cookies while you preheat the oven to 350°F (175°C).

11. Bake for 10 to 15 minutes or until the edges have slightly browned and the top has begun to firm up.

Tip: Odd-Shaped Sandwich Cookies

Sandwich cookies are easy if your cookie mold is round or square, or if it comes with its own cutter, as a few do. But what do you do if you want to make a sandwich cookie with an irregular-shaped mold?

Easy: Bake one cookie from your mold. Lay it face up on a sheet of parchment paper or thin plastic, and trace around it with a pencil.

Cut about a sixteenth inch inside the line. The cookie will expand a tiny bit as it bakes, so you want your pattern to be very slightly smaller than the cookie.

Now you have a template.

Using a sheet of nonstick foil for backing, roll out the dough you want to use for the bottom layer of the cookie. Chill it thoroughly and, using your template, cut out each cookie back with a sharp knife such as a craft knife. Remove the scraps and bake it as a test cookie to make sure the size is right.

Correct if necessary, and cut and bake enough cookie backs to make sandwiches with your molded cookies. You can trim the cookie backs slightly while they're still warm, if needed to fit the tops.

Just before serving, assemble the backs and tops with a filling.

FEBRUARY

Valentine Hearts, Flowers, and Chocolates

Poor St. Valentine! Removed from the Catholic Church's General Roman Calendar without so much as a Dear John letter!

It's not possible, though, to get rid of the idea of love. It renews everything, and spring reminds us of that renewal.

We may have mild winters or hard ones here on San Juan Island, but the first flowers of spring are equally welcome in either case. Crocuses pop up in my yard overnight, and it's the same every year—one morning, I look at the window to check for snow and see them instead.

That doesn't mean that cold weather is past, but it's a welcome sight for all that. And after crocuses, we get daffodils, tulips, narcissus, hyacinth, and others that I don't even know the names of. They smell wonderful. By the end of February, the cherry trees will be blooming...and the year begins again.

Decades ago, I had a grandmother who lived in Little Rock, Arkansas. Her house was on a large corner lot, and the cross street came through at an odd angle, so her yard was irregular in shape. She had planted every kind of daffodil and narcissus you can imagine, and as she got older, she let them go wild. In spring, the back yard was filled with thousands of blooms in every shade of white and yellow. The house is still there, but the flowers are gone. Except that they live on in my memory— a paradise of daffodils.

In addition to flowers, of course, we celebrate Valentine's Day with heart-shaped symbols. The origin of this shape isn't known, but everyone agrees that it goes back for centuries. Heart-shaped cookie molds are very common, possibly because molded cookies are so often made for someone who is loved.

And what better time to celebrate chocolate, as well! This month, we'll look at many versions of chocolate cookies—from white chocolate and mild cocoa flavors to the darkest possible chocolate. And for those who don't favor chocolate, there's a spice cookie and a special sugar cookie.

Recipe: Milk Chocolate Cherry Cookie Tartlets

Do you remember milk-chocolate-covered cherries? When I was first dating, that was the big-deal gift to get from a boyfriend on Valentine's Day. We've graduated to gourmet truffles now, and nostalgia, as they say, ain't what it used to be. Still, I remember the cherries fondly, and this cookie tart version is very good.

2 ounces (57 grams) baking chocolate

¾ cup (170 grams) unsalted butter

1 large egg

½ cup (100 grams) sugar

¼ cup (18 grams) nonfat dry milk

½ teaspoon salt

½ cup (118 milliliters) sweetened condensed milk. (See note.)

1 tablespoon cream

1 teaspoon vanilla extract

About 2 cups (280 grams) all-purpose flour (plain flour)

1. Warm the chocolate and butter together in a low oven or microwave until the chocolate is soft and the butter is melted. The chocolate may hold its shape when soft, so test with a spoon to avoid overcooking.

2. Stir the chocolate and butter together. Set aside.

3. Beat the egg in a large bowl until yolk and white are fully mixed.

4. Mix the sugar, nonfat dry milk, and salt.

5. Add the sugar mixture to the egg.

6. Mix the condensed milk, cream, and vanilla extract.

7. Add the milk mixture to the egg mixture.

8. Add flour slowly until the dough is solid enough to knead.

9. Knead in additional flour until the dough is the consistency of children's modeling clay.

10. Using a tart mold, press out cookie tart shells. (Complete illustrated directions for cookie tartlets are available at the beginning of this book.)

11. Bake the cookies at 350°F (175°C) for ten to twelve minutes.

12. Fill with cherry jam, cherry spread mixed with cream cheese, or cherry pie filling.

Notes

Sweetened condensed milk is NOT the same as evaporated milk. It's available just about everywhere, but you do have to check labels to make sure you have the right product.

Recipe: Dark Chocolate Cookies with Marzipan Topping

Valentine's Day demands chocolate, but chocolate and cookie molds aren't the best match in the world. If the chocolate is light enough that the pattern of the cookie is distinct, chocolate lovers are disappointed in the taste. There are many ways around this, and this recipe offers one more. It isn't actually a molded cookie. It's molded marzipan on a cookie. It's good. And surprisingly easy.

4 ounces (115 grams) baking chocolate
½ cup (115 grams) unsalted butter
1 large egg
¾ cup (150 grams) sugar
½ teaspoon salt
2 tablespoons baking cocoa
2 tablespoons black coffee
1 teaspoon vanilla extract
1 teaspoon chocolate extract
About 2 cups (280 grams) all-purpose flour (plain flour)
Chocolate frosting or chocolate spread (See note.)
Marzipan, either commercial or homemade

1. Warm the chocolate and butter together in a low oven or microwave until the chocolate is soft and the butter is melted. The chocolate may hold its shape when soft, so test with a spoon to avoid overcooking.

2. Stir the chocolate and butter together. Set aside.

3. Beat the egg in a large bowl until yolk and white are fully mixed.

4. Mix the sugar, salt, and cocoa. Sift to remove lumps.

5. Add the sugar mixture to the egg.

6. Add the coffee, vanilla extract, and chocolate extract to the egg mixture.

7. Add the chocolate mixture to the egg mixture.

8. Add flour slowly until the dough is solid enough to knead.

9. Knead in additional flour until the dough is the consistency of children's modeling clay.

10. Roll and form the marzipan toppings. (For directions, see the article following this recipe.)

11. Roll the cookie dough to a uniform thickness. Cut rectangles or circles larger than your molded marzipan toppings.

12. Bake the cookies at 350°F (175°C) for ten to twelve minutes.

13. Cool the cookies and spread with frosting, spread, or topping to help stick the marzipan to the cookie.

14. Center a marzipan topping piece on each cookie and press very lightly.

Notes

I used chocolate almond spread, but ice cream topping would also work.

Tip: Working with Marzipan

Marzipan is a mixture of ground almonds, sugar, and sometimes sugar syrup. If the texture is right, it's very easy to mold. If you make or buy marzipan that's too sticky, work in some sifted confectioner's sugar (icing sugar) until it is a little stiffer than children's modeling clay. If it's too dry, wrap it in a damp towel and microwave it for five seconds. I found I didn't need to prepare my cookie molds—the marzipan didn't stick to them. With different molds, the results might have been different, though.

If there are flaws in the design of the unmolded marzipan, you can use a water color brush, water, and a knife or clay tools to improve it. Cut excess off with a craft knife, and let the molded marzipan toppings dry a bit on a cookie cooling rack, if necessary.

Recipe: Cinnamon Cocoa Cookies

A spice cookie with a subtle chocolate flavoring. You can increase the chocolate and decrease the cinnamon to change the flavor balance.

> 1 cup (225 grams) unsalted butter
> 1 large egg
> ½ cup (120 milliliters) honey
> 1 teaspoon chocolate extract
> ½ teaspoon vanilla
> ½ cup (100 grams) sugar
> 1 tablespoon cinnamon
> 1 teaspoon cocoa
> ¼ teaspoon salt
> About 4 cups (560 grams) all-purpose flour (plain flour)

1. Melt the butter and set aside.
2. Beat the egg in a large bowl until yolk and white are fully mixed.

3. Mix the honey, chocolate extract, and vanilla extract. Add to the egg and beat until well mixed.

4. Mix the sugar, cocoa, cinnamon, and salt. Add to the egg mixture and beat until well mixed.

5. Add the melted butter slowly and beat until well mixed.

6. Add flour slowly until the mixture is solid enough to knead.

7. Transfer to your work surface and knead in more flour to make a soft, slightly sticky dough.

8. Wrap or cover the dough and refrigerate for up to ½ hour—until it's firm but still flexible.

9. Roll and form the dough.

10. Refrigerate the cookies while you preheat the oven to 350°F (175°C), or lower for especially thick cookies.

11. Bake for 10 to 15 minutes or until the edges have slightly browned and the top has begun to firm up.

Tip: Trimming Cookies

This mold has hearts at the bottom corners, which makes it appealing as a square cookie, but there are a couple of problems. The mold is very deep, so that it's difficult to bake the cookie properly if the background is included.  By the time the cupid's face is baked, the edges tend to be overcooked. Also, it makes a very large cookie, and—as you can see—it's not that easy to trim it straight. If I were doing it again,

I'd cut a square of parchment paper as a guide, or use a large square cookie cutter.

It's tempting to trim the dough flush with the cookie mold before you unmold the cookie—that will get you a straight edge every time. The problem is, it's harder to get the cookie out of the mold if you do. You have nothing to hang onto, and you don't have the weight of the extra dough pulling away from the mold. If you do this, you can often get the cookie started unmolding by pressing lightly at the edge, parallel to the face of the cookie, and pulling gently down as you do. Once you get the unmolding started, you have only to wait—the force of gravity is on your side.

The trimmed version is much easier, and either could be very attractive. The untrimmed one would be especially pretty if it were painted with cookie paint to make a real valentine.

Recipe: I-Love-You Cookies

The flavors are white chocolate, honey, raspberry, and rose. The measurements in this recipe give a subtle flavor. You can use more rose water if you prefer, but be careful, or your cookies will taste unpleasantly perfume-y. Very good served with fresh raspberries.

4 ounces (114 grams) white chocolate
4 ounces (114 grams) butter
1 large egg, beaten
½ cup (100 grams) sugar
¼ teaspoon salt
½ cup (120 milliliters) honey
2 tablespoons raspberry liqueur or syrup
1 tablespoon milk or cream
1 teaspoon rose water
½ teaspoon vanilla extract
About 4 cups (560 grams) all-purpose flour (plain flour)

1. Warm the chocolate and butter in a low oven or a microwave until the butter is melted and the chocolate is soft. The chocolate may hold its shape when softened, so test with a spoon when the butter is melted.

2. Stir the butter and chocolate together and set aside.

3. Beat the egg in a large bowl.

4. Mix sugar and salt. Add to the egg.

5. Mix the honey, raspberry liqueur, milk, rose water, milk, and vanilla extract. Add to the egg.

6. Slowly add the melted butter and chocolate.

7. Add flour slowly until the mixture is solid enough to knead. If you're using an electric mixer, stop the mixer once or twice as you're adding flour, and scrape the sides of the bowl to get all the flour mixed in.

8. Transfer the dough to a work surface and continue adding flour a little at a time until you have smooth, slightly sticky dough.

9. Roll and form the dough.

10. Chill the cookies while you preheat the oven to 320°F (160°C).

11. Bake for 10 minutes or until slightly browned at the edges.

Tip: Texture in Molded Cookies

For some people, the ideal cookie is a soft, gooey, cakey morsel. Those can be great. But molded cookies have to be a bit more solid than that—more like shortbread or gingersnaps.

Also delicious, just different.

For slightly cake-ier molded cookies, serve them warm.

Or go the other way: Make them thin, serve them at room temperature, and enjoy their crispness.

Or serve your cookies with fruit or ice cream, cocoa, tea, or coffee. Or mulled cider.

I do have a few cookie molds that seem to make cookies that are better to look at than to eat. For the most part, they're antique molds. These molds make large cookies, and often they're thick as well. This gives a chance for the cookie to have a beautiful design, but if you serve them, they're an awful lot of cookie for one person to eat. And of course, when you break them up, the beautiful design disappears.

It's a good idea to experiment with any mold/recipe combination before you serve it for a special occasion.

Recipe: Chocolate Orange Layer Cookies

1 cup (227 grams) butter

1 large egg

½ cup (120 milliliters) honey

2 teaspoons culinary orange oil. (See note.)

1 teaspoon natural orange flavoring

½ cup (98 grams) sugar

⅛ teaspoon salt

About 4½ (630 grams) cups all-purpose flour (plain flour)

2 tablespoons baking cocoa (See note.)

1. Melt the butter and set aside.

2. Beat the egg in a large bowl until yolk and white are fully mixed.

3. Mix the honey, orange oil, and orange flavoring. Add to the egg and beat until well mixed.

4. Mix the sugar and salt. Add to the egg mixture and beat until well mixed.

5. Add the melted butter slowly and beat until well mixed.

6. Add flour slowly until the mixture is almost solid enough to knead. Remove from the mixer and divide into two pieces, one about twice the size of the other.

7. Transfer the smaller piece to your work surface and knead in more flour to make a soft, slightly sticky dough.

8. Transfer the larger piece to your work surface and knead in the cocoa and enough flour to make a soft, slightly sticky dough.

9. Roll the dough in two layers as described in the January section of this book. The chocolate layer is the lower layer.

10. Form the cookies.

11. Refrigerate the cookies while you preheat the oven to 320°F (160°C).

12. Bake for 10 to 15 minutes or until the edges have slightly browned and the top has begun to firm up.

Notes

You may substitute 2 teaspoons of finely grated orange peel for the orange oil, but it will show as a speck in the cookie.

I recommend extra dark baking cocoa for maximum chocolate flavor. You may also add 1 tablespoon of shaved dark chocolate or finely chopped chocolate chips. If used, chocolate chips must be chopped finely enough that they won't poke through the pale top layer of dough and ruin the pattern.

Tip: Preparing Cookie Molds

A cookie mold that's properly prepared is one of the keys to success. But they're not all alike.

For most molds, I oil the surface of the mold very lightly, wiping off any oil that looks sparkly. The mold should have the kind of slight sheen that painters call "satin."

Then I use a fine-bristle pastry brush—Ateco makes a good one—to spread flour thinly over the surface of the dough.

The cookie almost always comes out of the mold beautifully, at least with my recipes.

However, a few molds just have to be different. Sometimes it's an unfinished wood mold or an unusually coarse pottery one.

If a difficult mold has very fine detail, I use just flour, no oil. The cookies will often have flour on the surface when they're unmolded, so I let them sit at room temperature until it's absorbed, usually about half an hour. You can also chill them and brush the flour off the surface. Some mold makers recommend powdered sugar or cornstarch for dusting molds. I prefer the flour, but you might prefer something else.

If the difficult mold has large flat areas, I use just oil, no flour. The molds that have needed this have always been coarse pottery molds, like terra cotta flowerpot material. I soak the surface with oil before using the mold, and let it sink in. Then I use it. So far, this has worked for me much better than dusting with flour.

The best thing to do is, try the main method first. A little oil on the mold, a little flour (or cornstarch or powdered sugar) on the dough. If this doesn't work, experiment.

Recipe: Sweets-for-the-Sweet Sugar Cookies

1 cup (227 grams) butter
1 large egg
1 tablespoon milk
1 tablespoon white corn syrup
1 teaspoon vanilla extract
1 cup (200 grams) sugar
¼ teaspoon salt
About 4⅛ cups (575 grams) all-purpose flour (plain
   flour)

1. Melt the butter and set aside.
2. Beat the egg in a large bowl until yolk and white are fully mixed.

3. Mix the milk, corn syrup, and vanilla extract. Add to the egg and beat until well mixed.

4. Mix the sugar and salt. Add to the egg mixture and beat until well mixed.

5. Add the melted butter slowly and beat until well mixed.

6. Add flour slowly until the mixture is solid enough to knead.

7. Transfer to your work surface and knead in more flour to make a soft, slightly sticky dough.

8. Wrap or cover the dough and refrigerate for up to ½ hour—until it's firm but still flexible.

9. Roll and form the dough.

10. Refrigerate the cookies while you preheat the oven to 350°F (175°C), or lower for especially thick cookies.

11. Bake for 10 to 15 minutes or until the edges have slightly browned and the top has begun to firm up.

Tip: Cookie Molds from Found Objects

Suppose you have something that looks like it might work as a cookie mold—but it isn't one. You might be curious enough to try it.

And it might work. But be sure it's a food safe material, and that it doesn't have a bad taste—brass, for example, tastes pretty bad, unless it's lacquered. Many objects are fairly easy to use for molding cookies—just roll out the dough, brush it with flour, and press your "mold" into it firmly. Then cut

out your cookies with a pastry wheel, cookie cutter, or knife. Or lay another cookie mold lightly over the molded dough and use it as an outline guide. I can't speak for anyone else's recipes, but it works fine with mine.

The candy dish I show in the photo above is one that caught my eye. Both the top and the bottom are fancy-cut glass, and it looked like it might have potential.

It's a dish with its own story. This one is about my other grandmother—not the daffodil one.

She was a very proper old lady when I knew her, and if family stories are true, she was proper even when she was young. Many years after she was gone, my father gave me this candy dish, which had been hers. I didn't need a candy dish, but I loved the story he told me about it.

It seems my grandfather had to travel during the Depression to earn a living. Since he had to leave his wife and children at home, he bought my grandmother a gun. She kept it in the candy dish. It's not a very large dish, so it must have been a small gun. She never used it, never needed to.

But the idea of my ladylike grandmother with a Saturday night special amuses me so much that I'll cherish the dish forever. It works pretty well as a cookie mold, too.

MARCH

Saint Patrick's Day and Shortbread

Here on San Juan Island, March can bring just about anything—sunshine and flowers, rain, or fierce windstorms that scatter the cherry blossoms like snow. One day, the sea will be blue and sparkling; the next, it's gray and sullen. Spring is here, except when it's not.

The threat of serious winter storms is over, but we can still find snow dusting the blooming tulips. Sometimes, the rhododendron flowers last only a day or two before the wind shreds them. It's hard to know what to expect. We keep an eye on the forecast, noting how fast it changes. We dress in layers and hope for the best.

This month's cookie molds feature traditional symbols of the British Isles, the homeland of shortbread. And of St. Patrick, whose day is celebrated this month. Patrick is credited, among other things, with driving the snakes out of Ireland, though science maintains there were never any there to begin with.

More certain is the attribution to Patrick of a version of a prayer called "St. Patrick's Breastplate" or "The Deer's Cry," a beautiful poem often beautifully sung. Patrick is also associated with the shamrock, which he supposedly used as a teaching tool. The thistle of Scotland, rose of England, Celtic knot, and Irish harp complete the themes of this month's cookie molds.

May the road rise up to meet you.
May the wind always be at your back.
May the sun shine warm upon your face,
and rains fall soft upon your fields.

—Old Irish blessing

Perhaps Patrick would not have known shortbread, or wouldn't have eaten it if he had. That might have been just as well. When it comes to shortbread, feelings can run high, which would detract from monastic calm.

People who love shortbread know exactly what they want. The problem is, they don't all want the same thing. Desirable shortbread qualities include—depending on who you ask—flaky, buttery, soft, delicate, caramelized, and crisp. It's possible to make shortbread with several of these qualities, but not all. Your choice of mold and ingredients will be the key to getting the shortbread you want.

Traditional ingredients are butter, flour, and sugar—that's all. The flour may include oat or rice flour as well as wheat. But there are many variations and additions, some for taste, others for workability. These include vanilla or other flavorings, ground nuts, spelt flour, confectioner's sugar, cocoa powder in place of some of the flour, eggs or egg yolks, water, cream, baking powder, and more.

Shortbread as we know it today was probably first made in Scotland. Traditionally, it was hand-formed as a round flat cake with a crimped edge. Probably later, shortbread was also made as fingers, which were narrow rectangles, and as small rounds. It was often pricked with a fork over the top surface. All these shapes were baked on a flat pan.

Since shortbread wasn't traditionally a molded cookie, it's not the easiest cookie to mold. It is very tender, and is likely to break when you unmold it. It also, more than most cookie dough, tends to puff and distort in the oven. And it tends to hold details through baking less well than most cookie dough.

Commercial shortbread cookies are formed with mechanical rollers, and are thinner and crisper than the shortbread usually made by home cooks. It's possible for these rollers to impress a pattern on the cookies, and some firms do this, though others duplicate the simpler traditional shapes, including the fork punctures. They're baked on flat pans or sheets, like traditional homemade shortbread. The closest thing to these rollers that would be available to a home cook can use is a springerle rolling pin. I've never seen one suggested for shortbread, but actually, they do an excellent job with it. And since they minimize handling, you get less fuss and breakage than with most traditional shortbread molds.

I'm not a fan of the pottery pans for baking shortbread with a molded pattern on the bottom, but I have figured out one way to get them to work fairly well, which I'll share with you later in this March section.

Tip: Creating Your Own Shortbread Recipes

I could create a few shortbread recipes, or a book full of them. Instead, I want to look at shortbread as a method and give you the tools for creating your own.

Here are the ingredients I use in shortbread:

Sugar: Any kind—white, brown, maple, whatever. It should be finely granulated. Artificial sweeteners aren't going to work here.

My recipe calls for ½ cup, which is 100 grams for white sugar. If you're using another kind, you'll need to find the equivalent weight to ½ cup.

Syrup: This isn't traditional, but it makes a big difference in how easily your cookies unmold. Since shortbread is probably the least cooperative of all molded cookies, I shrug at tradition and use 1 tablespoon of syrup. This can be honey, molasses, sieved jam or jelly, agave syrup, corn syrup, maple syrup, or probably a host of others. I haven't tried everything, but pancake syrup, syrups intended for coffee flavoring, chocolate syrup, coconut cream, or a dozen others would probably work. The purpose of the syrup is to help the cookies hang together well enough to unmold.

Flour: About 2½ cups (350 grams) of flour. Up to a half cup of this may be a flour substitute, such as rice flour or cocoa. If the cookie molds are small and simple, up to 50% of the flour can be cake flour.

You can use about 2 ounces, or 60 grams, of nuts as part of the flour amount. If you use nuts, you'll probably have to grind them yourself. The way I do this is to toast them lightly, remove the skins if necessary, and process them in a food processor with one cup of the flour. The flour keeps the nuts from turning into nut butter.

Regarding the skins of nuts: Some nuts don't have them. For others, such as pecans, it doesn't matter. Almonds should be blanched. You can usually buy them that way, but you can also blanch them yourself. Hazelnuts should be toasted, and the skins rubbed off with a coarse cloth.

Flavorings: Traditionally, none are used. If you decide to be non-traditional, the sky is the limit. Consider flavoring extracts, culinary flavoring oils, ground lavender buds, grated fresh ginger, ground spices, or anything else that appeals to you. I often use the book *The Flavor Bible*, by Karen Page and Andrew Dornenburg. I've always been pleased with their recommendations—it's a great resource.

Baking: I like a temperature of 320°F (160°C) for shortbread—a little lower than I'd use for most cookies. Keep an eye on the cookies, as they burn easily. They're done when the bottoms are browned. Remove them from the oven if you're not sure whether they're done—it won't hurt anything if you have to put them back for a few minutes.

Fillings: If you use a cookie tart mold, you can fill the shortbread cookies with dabs of lemon curd, frosting, whipped cream, whipped cream cheese, jam, nut butters, or combinations of these.

Accompaniments: Fresh fruit is good with shortbread. So is ice cream, or whipped cream. Marry the flavors so it all works together.

Tip: Molding Shortbread

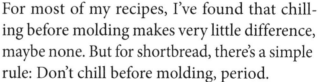

For most of my recipes, I've found that chilling before molding makes very little difference, maybe none. But for shortbread, there's a simple rule: Don't chill before molding, period.

Here's what happens when you bake a cookie: The butterfat melts. The sugar melts. The flour and water have combined during mixing, and they become a solid structure. So do the eggs, if any.

In shortbread, the water content of the butter combines with the flour to provide the structure. But the butterfat and sugar content is so high that the cookie will run if the dough was stiff enough to mold only because the butterfat was chilled. Instead, you must add enough flour to make a molding consistency at room temperature.

If your cookies are small, you can make the cookies tenderer by using pastry flour, half cake flour and half all-purpose, or US Southern all-purpose flour such as White Lily. However, if you use a soft flour with a too-large cookie mold, the cookies will crack.

Shortbread Pans

Traditionally, shortbread was rolled like pie crust, sometimes marked with a fork, and baked without being molded or decorated in any way. Shortbread molds are relatively recent. The earliest shortbread mold I've seen, one from the early twentieth century, reproduces a large, crimped round, another traditional shape.

In the late twentieth century, several firms began making ceramic or metal pans with have fancy patterns such as Scottish thistles, flowers, hearts, or even animals. The shortbread is baked in the pans, removed, and sliced into individual servings while it's still warm.

Problems with Shortbread Pans

I don't know anyone who is completely satisfied with ceramic or metal shortbread pan molds. I've tried different patterns, different brands, different recipes, different oven temperatures, different you-name-it, and the result is always one or another version of the same story: The cookie heaves, bubbles, and distorts during baking. Sometimes you can tell what the pattern was supposed to be, sometimes you can't.

Even when this problem is minimized, so that most of the pattern is replicated, the texture of the molded side is quite coarse—well, after all, it *is* the bottom of the cookie!

Every tester who has worked with me has had the same experience with bake-in pans and molds, and I'm ready to say: These cookie molds just don't seem to have much potential to produce beautiful cookies.

It annoys me that some online booksellers pair these molds with my books, because *Baking with Cookie Molds* clearly says that most of these pans don't work well. I have no control at all over their pairings, so there's nothing I can do about it.

Working with Shortbread Pans

I got my best results by using multiple pie weight chains on top of the dough as it was baking, to minimize the bubbling and heaving. I used a round of parchment paper between the weights and the dough to keep the weights from sinking in. It definitely improved the look of the cookies, but I still regarded the results as far from ideal.

Other cookie dough besides shortbread can be baked in these pans with slightly better results, especially if the cookies are no thicker than about ¼ inch. (Thinner shortbread had better results than thicker, as well.)

Of course, you can use them like other cookie molds—form the cookies in them and bake on a cookie sheet. If you do this, do one segment at a time.

I think my mom had the best solution—she used her shortbread pan as a serving dish for cookies she made with other molds.

There is one exception to the generally dismal results I've gotten with bake-in molds. The cookie shown above was baked in a different kind of cookie molding pan, one made of silicone.

With these, using my method with pie weights, the results have been far better. The only drawback is that they're not available in many patterns.

Shortbread with Other Cookie Molds

Most people are happier with their molded shortbread if they use pottery or wood cookie stamps, or roller-type or board-type springerle molds. This is completely non-traditional as a home method, although it more or less duplicates the way commercial shortbread cookies have always been made. Rollers produce a crisper cookie, and the outer surface may taste somewhat caramelized, which is delicious.

Recipe: Tropical Shortbread

My Scottish grandma had a wicked sense of humor—I'm trying to imagine what she'd have had to say about such an unorthodox recipe. Whatever she'd have said, though, she'd have had a twinkle in her eyes, and I suspect she would have had a few of the cookies, too.

1 cup (225 grams) butter
½ cup (100 grams) sugar
1 tablespoon honey
1 teaspoon grated fresh ginger
¼ teaspoon culinary tangerine or orange oil
½ teaspoon grated lemon peel
½ cup (80 grams) finely ground roasted unsalted cashews
   (See note.)
2 cups (280 grams) all-purpose flour (plain flour)

1. Cream the butter, sugar, and honey.

2. Combine the ginger, tangerine oil, and lemon peel, and add to the butter mixture.

3. Add flour and ground nuts slowly until the mixture is solid enough to knead.

4. Transfer to your work surface and knead in all but the last ¼ cup (35 grams) of all-purpose flour (plain flour).

5. Add up to ¼ cup (35 grams) more flour slowly and carefully, checking the texture of your dough as you go. Stop adding when the dough is still tacky but no longer sticks to your work surface.

6. When the flour amount seems right, wrap and set aside. Do not chill before molding.

7. I recommend molding and baking a test cookie to make sure your dough is correct. If you haven't added enough flour, the cookies won't hold an impression.

8. Preheat the oven to 320°F (160°C).

9. Bake the test cookie for 10 to 15 minutes or until the edges have slightly browned and the top has begun to firm up.

10. Examine the test cookie. If it has spread during baking and the design has become blurry, knead a little more flour into the rest of the dough and repeat the test.

11. When you have good results from the test, form and bake the rest of the cookies.

Notes

To grind cashews, combine the nuts with about one cup of the flour and grind in a food processor with a steel blade until the nuts are finely ground.

To get more of the subtle cashew flavor, use less of the ginger, tangerine, and lemon, or eliminate them completely. Either way, delicious and different!

Recipe: Chocolate Almond Shortbread

I made this cookie with a mold that creates a tart shape. You can use smaller tart molds as well. It's filled with chopped almonds and garnished with lines of chocolate syrup.

1 cup (225 grams) butter
½ cup (100 grams) sugar
1 tablespoon dark chocolate syrup
1 teaspoon vanilla
½ teaspoon almond extract
2 tablespoons dark cocoa powder
2¼ cups (315 grams) all-purpose flour (plain flour)

1. Cream the butter, sugar, and chocolate syrup.

2. Add the vanilla extract and almond extract.

3. Add cocoa. Add flour slowly until the mixture is solid enough to knead.

4. Transfer to your work surface and knead in all but the last ¼ cup (35 grams) of flour.

5. Add up to ¼ cup (35 grams) more flour slowly and carefully, checking the texture of your dough as you go. Stop adding when the dough is still tacky but no longer sticks to your work surface.

6. When the flour amount seems right, wrap and set aside. Do not chill before molding.

7. I recommend molding and baking a test cookie to make sure your dough is correct. If you haven't added enough flour, the cookies won't hold an impression.

8. Preheat the oven to 320°F (160°C).

9. Bake the test cookie for 10 to 15 minutes or until the edges have slightly browned and the top has begun to firm up.

10. Examine the test cookie. If it has spread during baking and the design has become blurry, knead a little more flour into the rest of the dough and repeat the test.

11. When you have good results from the test, form and bake the rest of the cookies.

Recipe: Butterscotch Shortbread

I show these as unfilled shells, but they could be filled with butterscotch ice cream topping, chopped pecans (which you'd bake in the shells), maple cream, chocolate buttercream, or any number of other goodies.

 1 cup (225 grams) butter
 ¼ cup (50 grams) white sugar
 ¼ cup (50 grams) packed dark brown sugar
 1 teaspoon vanilla extract
 1 teaspoon butterscotch flavoring
 2½ cups (350 grams) all-purpose flour

 1. Cream the butter and sugar.
 2. Add the vanilla extract and butterscotch flavoring to the butter mixture.
 3. Add flour slowly until the mixture is solid enough to knead.
 4. Transfer to your work surface and knead in all but the last ¼ cup (35 grams) of all-purpose flour (plain flour).

5. Add up to ¼ cup (35 grams) more flour slowly and carefully, checking the texture of your dough as you go. Stop adding when the dough is still tacky but no longer sticks to your work surface.

6. When the flour amount seems right, wrap and set aside. Do not chill before molding.

7. I recommend molding and baking a test cookie to make sure your dough is correct. If you haven't added enough flour, the cookies won't hold an impression.

8. Preheat the oven to 320°F (160°C).

9. Bake the test cookie for 10 to 15 minutes or until the edges have slightly browned and the top has begun to firm up.

10. Examine the test cookie. If it has spread during baking and the design has become blurry, knead a little more flour into the rest of the dough and repeat the test.

11. When you have good results from the test, form and bake the rest of the cookies.

Tip: The Perfect Traditional Shortbread

What got me started on a quest for perfect shortbread was comparing my mom's non-molded shortbread with my own molded version. Mine was prettier, but—hands down—hers was more tender, melt-in-your-mouth. I wondered why I couldn't have both.

After a lot of experimenting, I found I really *couldn't* have 100% of both. The reason is that the structure that makes a molded cookie hold its shape comes mostly from the protein, or gluten, content of the flour. My mom's shortbread is tender because she uses "soft," or low-gluten, flour.

To get down to specifics, she uses a brand from the U.S. South, White Lily flour. White Lily is about 7% protein. In the US, cake flour, depending on brand, is 5% to 8% protein. Pastry flour is 8% to 9%. All-purpose is 9% to 12%. A note of caution: Flour varies a lot from one country to another, so if you're thinking about really calculating how to make ideal shortbread, you should look at the flour package to see what you have.

If you don't want to get into math, though, here's how to wing it. If 7% is ideal, you can experiment. If your all-purpose flour (plain flour) is 10%, try mixing half and half with cake flour. With a dough this tender, you have to use small, uncomplicated molds.

Experiment a bit to get a cookie that combines your preferences for texture and appearance.

APRIL

Easter Baskets

While we children slept, the Easter Bunny would leave baskets by our beds. They were colorful baskets, already half-full of gifts—wire-footed chenille chicks nested in shiny cellophane grass, tiny chocolate eggs that looked like robin eggs, and colorful boxes with windows that revealed sugar "peep eggs"—which is what we called panorama eggs—and chocolate bunnies or chickens. And the most wonderful thing of all, waiting beside the baskets, were our plush Easter bunnies—or sometimes other animals. I vividly remember a swan with a music box inside.

As soon as we woke, we'd go out, my older sister and I, into the early, early morning, and look for the goodies the Bunny had hidden in the yard. I've always loved dawn—maybe this is one reason why. And why I still like baskets, too.

I grew up in New Orleans, so early spring mornings weren't usually cold. But there must have been years when it rained on Easter. Surely the Bunny must have hidden the eggs in the house occasionally. But my rose-colored glasses will only focus on spring sunshine and morning dew, birds chirping, and the bright colors of Easter eggs waiting in the grass and among the flowers.

Finding those eggs was fun for its own sake, because I don't care to *eat* hardboiled eggs—never have. So the finding was the only treasure, but it was no less special for that. I also didn't like the hard marshmallow candy eggs and was fairly indifferent to jelly beans, though the bright colors were just right for Easter. But the chocolate-covered eggs and—best of all—the pecan nougat ones were another matter. My favorite fillings in the chocolate eggs were pineapple, coconut, and cherry. So I've worked out some cookie recipes this month with all those flavors, and with pecan and chocolate, too.

My sister and I would keep the milk chocolate animals for weeks, until they were no longer special, and then nibble at them till they were gone. And finally, regretfully, the panorama eggs, which wouldn't last through a humid New Orleans summer and actually didn't taste good, as they were nothing but sugar. We could have thrown them away, but somehow that seemed too cavalier, too unappreciative of the Bunny and his gifts. The toy bunnies were treasured "forever," or at least a couple of years. That's as good as forever, when you're two and four years old.

Years later, I got to be the Bunny's helper for my much-younger brother, and I enjoyed that even more. Dyeing eggs in the kitchen after his bedtime, trying all the pretty colors and variations I could get by dipping the eggs twice. Getting up before dawn with instructions about how well I could hide them—the point being, as the Bunny explained, not to outsmart my brother but to amuse him. So I'd make sure the concealment was age-appropriate, and help him a little if I'd been just a little too clever. The Bunny was pretty definite about not wanting a yard full of rotten eggs—an understandable position.

Here on San Juan Island, the Fire Department plays Bunny for the children, hiding the eggs—plastic ones—in the sea grass and driftwood of the shore. The eggs are redeemed for candy and toys at a prize table.

It's a long way in time, distance, and feeling from New Orleans dawns with my sister. But kids are still celebrating, and adults are still having fun helping them do it. Some things really do last forever.

As you know by now, I use honey or other liquid sweeteners in my recipes to make them easier to unmold. For this month, though, we're going to explore the use of sugar, and adjusting sugar and liquid sweetener proportions to suit our mold. We're going to do a little decorating, too. And finally—one month for shortbread just wasn't enough—we'll have strawberry shortbread for Easter dinner.

Tip: Recognizing Kinds of Cookie Molds

This is important if you want to modify recipes, as we'll be doing this month.

Cookie molds come to us from several different traditions. Springerle cookies are made in a tradition that used sugar as the sweetener. The mold is a flat surface—the old ones are boards, or boards covered with metal. Sometimes this surface might be curved into a rolling pin. This surface of a springerle mold has a design carved into it, but not a whole cookie. You have to cut the cookie out. Or, if the mold makes more than one design, you cut the cookies apart. A springerle mold works in about the same way a rubber stamp does.

The other main tradition is gingerbread or speculaas. These molds were originally used to make honey-sweetened cookies. The mold shapes the entire cookie. When you're finished molding the cookie, you have to pull it out of the mold. It has its own edges, just like something you make from a gelatin mold. You trim it, but the shape and edges are set by the mold. A gingerbread mold is like a very, very shallow gelatin or pudding mold. Today, these molds are called cavity molds.

Which type of mold you have makes a big difference in how easy it is to make cookies. Sugar is harder to handle than honey, because sugar dough is a collection of crumbs. It falls apart easily, and is very difficult to unmold from some cavity molds. So with this kind of dough, springerle molds are easier to use than cavity molds.

My book *Baking with Cookie Molds* concentrated on making molded cookies available to everyone, no matter what kind of molds they might have. For this month, we're going a step farther. We're going to get a little more advanced and see what we can get away with. Because there's no doubt that many people today do prefer the taste and texture of sugar-sweetened cookies to that of honey-sweetened ones. So we're going to use springerle molds to make sugar-sweetened butter cookies. And we'll look at how much honey you really need for cookies in different cavity molds.

So sort your molds, and separate the springerle molds from the cavity molds. Here's an illustration of each type.

First is a springerle mold, made by Springerle Joy. It's a flat surface with a pattern cut into it. You press it onto the dough and then cut out the cookie.

Springerle molds are easy to use because the dough doesn't have to be lifted or pulled from the mold. Usually, they are simple shapes, and the cookies can be cut out with ordinary cookie cutters.

Springerle molds tend to be small, and in some cases, the design is shallow.

Next is a cavity mold, made by Gene Wilson of HOBI Cookie Molds. The entire cookie shape is cut into the board. You press the dough into it and then unmold and trim the cookie.

Cavity molds can make large, dramatic cookies. The disadvantage of cavity molds is that it isn't always easy to get the cookie out of the mold.

Recognizing which cavity molds are easier and which require more advanced skills is a big help as you're learning to use them. If you're new to molded cookies, or to working with cavity molds, it's probably best to start with molds that don't have complicated designs or difficult shapes.

What would be a complicated design? One with a great deal of fine or deep texture, especially if the mold is unfinished wood or coarse pottery.

What would be a difficult shape? The most difficult shape would be one with inward-pointing angles—a star is a good example.

The mold illustrated above takes a bit of skill and patience. It's long and thin and has several inward-pointing angles—at the places where the basket meets the rabbit's back, at the back of the ears, and at the V shape made by the hind legs. If you know that a bit of gentle persuasion will be needed at these points, you're a long way ahead.

Recipe: Coconut Sugar Cookies

This is a cavity mold, yet I made the cookies successfully without using honey. This mold isn't a complicated design, and it isn't a difficult shape.

    1 cup (225 grams) unsalted butter
    1 large egg
    1 cup (200 grams) sugar
    1 tablespoon milk or cream
    1 tablespoon honey, optional
    2 teaspoons coconut extract
    ½ teaspoon vanilla extract
    ⅛ teaspoon salt
    About 4 cups (560 grams) all-purpose flour (plain flour)

1. Melt the butter and set aside.

2. Beat the egg in a large bowl until the yolk and white are fully mixed.

3. Mix the sugar and salt and add to the egg. Beat until well mixed.

4. Mix the milk, honey, coconut extract, and vanilla extract, and add to the egg mixture.

5. Add the melted butter slowly and beat until well mixed. Don't just pour it in quickly—the heat still in the butter could cook the egg!

6. Add flour slowly and mix in until you have dough that is solid enough to knead.

7. Transfer the dough to a floured work surface. Continue adding flour by kneading in a little at a time until the dough is smooth and slightly sticky.

8. Roll and form the dough.

9. Bake for 10 to 15 minutes or until the edges have slightly browned and the top has begun to firm up.

Notes

Honesty compels me to admit that this cookie was "decorated" in my photo app. As it turned out, it was the only way I could do it. By the time it occurred to me how cute it would look if it was painted, the real cookie had been eaten! But you could easily do something like this with cookie paints—if your family doesn't beat you to the cookies.

Recipe: Cherry and Chocolate Layer Cookies

Make the recipe above for Coconut Sugar Cookies, substituting cherry flavoring for the coconut extract.

Divide the dough in two. One piece should be about twice the size of the other. Into the smaller ball of dough, knead

    2 tablespoons mini chocolate chips
    2 tablespoons very finely chopped dried cherries

The cherries are going to expand quite a bit as they absorb liquid from the dough, so make sure the pieces are extra small. The cookies will be hard to cut out if you have pieces of dried fruit that are too large.

Now follow the instructions for layer cookies in the January section of this book.

Tip: Honey and Sugar—
The Pros and Cons

Many people today prefer the taste of sugar-sweetened cookies. Not everyone, though. Some of the testers who worked with me on the book still mention that their favorite thing about my cookies was that they weren't as sweet as modern cookies. But if you do like for sweets to be very sweet, that's the main advantage of using all sugar.

The disadvantage, in addition to possible problems unmolding the cookies, is that the dough dries out faster in handling, and rerolled dough is more likely to crack in the oven. It's just less flexible than dough that contains a fair amount of honey.

Try both, and see what you think. Then adjust my recipes—or anyone's—to suit your own taste.

Tip: Honey and Sugar—
Getting the Right Proportions

If you want sweeter, tenderer cookies than you get with honey-sweetened cookie recipes, you might be pleased with the results of maximizing the sugar. Learning what you can get away with is going to take some trial and error.

The higher the proportion of sugar in the recipe, the more fragile the dough will be. With a springerle board or a very easy cavity mold, you can get all the way to 100% sugar sweetening. If I do that, I prepare the molds a little differently. I use no oil, but dust both the mold and the dough lightly with flour, using a pastry brush to make a thin, even coat.

I like to use half sugar and half honey for a typical cavity mold.

Making cookies in enormous molds will be much easier if you use 100% honey instead. By "enormous," I mean something at least eight inches in diameter. I've make cookies almost two feet square, and gotten them perfect on the first try, with 100% honey dough. To modern tastes, an all-honey cookie is a little strange to eat, I must admit. It's denser than cookies today, and not all that sweet. However, enormous cookies aren't really expected to be gourmet quality.

The larger the mold, the more honey you'll need. If a mold is much larger in one direction than another, like a long rectangle, you may need more honey, too.

Tip: Strawberry Shortcake for Easter Dinner

To the Scottish part of my family, the idea of making strawberry shortcake with sponge cake or pound cake is anathema. Shortcake is made with shortbread, they say. I must admit, it's very good.

The secret to making shortbread in a large mold, like this one by Hartstone, is that you don't use the soft flour you can get away with using for tiny cookies. No, you're going to have to use regular all-purpose flour (plain flour) for a large

shortbread cookie. And—speaking of honey and sugar—adding just one tablespoon of honey to the traditional shortbread recipe will make it a lot easier to handle.

Another thing: Since these shortbread "pans" don't bake shortbread all that well, it's best to use the pan as if it were a large springerle mold, to shape your shortbread. Then bake it on a cookie sheet. I made a ring, rather like a flan ring, from nonstick aluminum foil and fastened it with a safety pin—this kept the cookie from spreading.

Of course, being confined in a ring made it want to puff. So I took it out of the oven several times while it was baking. This took the puff out, and let the cookie firm up a little. Then I put it back in the oven.

My husband and I like yogurt with our shortcake, but of course you could put whipped cream on it instead. If you're skilled with a decorating bag—which I'm not—you could probably do something very impressive.

Recipe: Chocolate Sugar Cookies

These cookies have their advantages and disadvantages. First of all, the main advantage—they're soft and cakelike, but still keep the molded pattern. Now the downside: They are harder to unmold. Just the same, the usual texture of molded cookies is something not everyone likes.

If you're interested in making your cookies this way, I suggest reading about the creaming method in Alton Brown's book *I'm Just Here for More Food*. He describes the best way to do it in very clear, detailed instructions. This is a modification of his recommendations, but I learned a lot by reading his book, and recommend it highly.

    1 cup (225 grams) unsalted butter, at room temperature
    1 cup (200 grams) sugar
    1 large egg at room temperature
    1 tablespoon milk or cream
    1 teaspoon vanilla extract
    2 teaspoons chocolate extract
    3¾ cups (525 grams) all-purpose flour (plain flour)
    2 tablespoons baking cocoa
    ⅛ teaspoon salt

1. Beat the butter briefly with the flat paddle of a stand mixer, at the lowest speed.

2. Increase the speed a little and trickle the sugar in gradually. Beat until light in color and texture.

3. Beat the egg and add to the butter and sugar.

4. Mix the milk, chocolate extract, and vanilla extract.

5. Mix the flour, salt, and cocoa

6. Add thirds of the flour mixture slowly, alternating with halves of the milk mixture.

7. Transfer the dough to a floured work surface. You may need to work in a little more flour to make dough that is smooth and slightly sticky.

8. Roll and form the dough. With this dough, I recommend lightly flouring both the dough and the mold rather than using oil. I find it helpful to roll dough on nonstick foil or baking parchment. Form the cookies from the rolled dough and trim the excess around them. It minimizes handling, and handling is what toughens the cookies.

9. Chill this dough before trimming the cookies. It won't trim neatly unless you do.

10. Bake for 10 to 15 minutes or until the edges have slightly browned and the top has begun to firm up.

Variation: Soft Chocolate Cookie Tartlets

I've also made the soft chocolate sugar cookies with a tart mold, and filled it with buttercream with the flavors of my long-ago-favorite candy eggs. Fill the cookie tartlets at the last minute to make sure they don't get soggy from the filling. Serve with fresh fruit.

Tip: Another Idea for Cookie Tartlets

Here's a plain shortbread—but you could make any molded cookie you want—made into a tart form with a pecan half used as a filling. You could make a chocolate dough, or butterscotch, or maple—any flavor you fancy. The filling doesn't have to be pecans—most unsalted nuts would be good. You make the tartlets, press the nut into the center, and bake them together. The nut toasts nicely while the cookie bakes.

If you use hazelnuts, remove the skins first. Keep an eye on the nuts to make sure they don't burn. If you are using almonds, try to get them already blanched.

Tip: Creatively Combining Cookie Molds and Cutters

Want to cut out a molded cookie but don't have a cookie cutter in the right size and shape? A little creativity can come in handy. In other words, you can fake it!

Here I'm cutting out an oval molded cookie with a round cookie cutter. You can cut a rectangle with a square cookie cutter in pretty much the same way. You just use part of the cutter at a time.

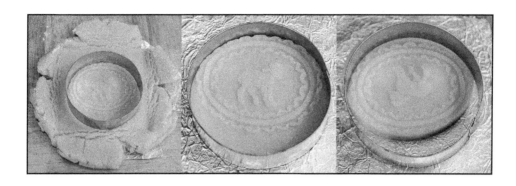

Russian Easter Egg Cookies

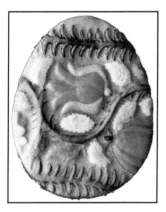

Some springerle molds create a pattern rather than an image. Here are cookies made with one of the all-over pattern rolling pins featured in the January section of this book, cut out with an egg-shaped cutter. You could paint these to resemble traditional Russian Easter eggs.

The picture shows my attempt at the coloring of a Russian Easter egg. Not quite Fabergé yet, but pretty just the same.

Panorama Egg Cookies

And here's one more bit of fun—a combination of a cookie stamp and an egg-shaped cutter. I made cookie "panorama egg" with this combination. The stamp makes the pattern and the round "hole," and you use the cutter to make the shape. Stamp first, then cut, or the cookie will distort.

With a little color and frosting, you could do something like in this picture.

Recipe: Pecan Cookies with Chocolate Backing

The nuts make the dough a little more difficult to handle, so I've used a larger amount of honey here. Whether you need that would depend partly on your mold.

    1 cup (225 grams) butter
    1 large egg
    ¼ cup (60 milliliters) honey
    ¾ cup (175 grams) sugar
    ½ cup (80 grams) finely ground pecans
    ¼ teaspoon salt
    About 4¼ cups (560 grams) all-purpose flour (plain
        flour)

1. Melt the butter. Set aside.
2. Beat the egg in a large bowl.
3. Add the honey to the egg mixture.
4. Mix the sugar, ground nuts, and salt. Add to the egg mixture.
5. Add the butter slowly and beat well.

6. Add flour slowly until the mixture is solid enough to knead. If you're using an electric mixer, stop the mixer once or twice as you're adding flour, and scrape the sides of the bowl to get all the flour mixed in.

7. Transfer to a counter and knead in a little more flour if required to make a soft, slightly sticky dough.

8. Wrap and refrigerate the dough for 30 minutes.

9. Roll and form the dough.

10. Chill the cookies while you preheat the oven to 350°F (177°C).

11. Bake for 10 to 15 minutes or until slightly browned at the edges.

12. For the chocolate backing, see the January section of this book.

MAY

Gardens, Flowers, Birds, and a Few Bugs

The gardening season has finally come to San Juan Island. Looking out my kitchen window, it's hard to believe the yard was so full of snow only a few weeks ago.

I've lived in many parts of the United States, and I always notice other people's gardens. I've had quite a few of my own, as well. Everywhere I've lived, there were wonderful things growing, and also things that wouldn't grow. When I was a child in New Orleans, two things I'd read about but never seen were lilacs and peonies. Probably the summers were too hot for them. I saw them for the first time when I lived in Olympia, Washington, and was as astonished as if I'd met a unicorn.

But New Orleans certainly had its gardens. Roses bloomed almost all year. And there were flowers I've never seen anywhere else—Magnolia fuscata, a small yellow magnolia with a banana liqueur scent. Actual bananas, too, and as a child, I thought there was nothing unusual about growing bananas in the back yard. And an elusive one that took me ages to find—sweet olive, Osmanthus fragrans. I'd walk down a block and smell apricot, look for flowers or fruit on the plants around me, and see nothing. Finally I found it: a sleek shrub with white flowers no bigger than a raisin. It was unbelievable that something so tiny could cast so much perfume into the air.

And the tomatoes! Louisiana Creole tomatoes were the best I've ever had. I don't eat tomatoes much, since I left the South.

Here on the island, my neighbors have sunny-looking plants—marigolds or zinnias, maybe. Lavender grows like a weed, and wild roses sprawl on empty land. Other kinds of roses require a lot of work to keep mildew away, though some people succeed with them. Fruit trees are everywhere—mostly pear and cherry, as far as I can tell.

Gardens aren't just plants, of course—they're full of birds. We have lovely hummingbirds here—iridescent gold. I mistook them for beetles at first. The only hummingbirds I'd seen up till then were ruby throats, which are beautiful too. I've seen all sorts of birds—goldfinches, robins, crows, swans, even bald eagles. And of course, many I can't identify, since I'm not a real birdwatcher. I make up names for them: this one's a Yellow-Legged Handrail Hopper, that one's a Short-Tail Screecher.

Of all the birds in New Orleans, I most remember the mockingbirds. My sister and I saved a baby one when we were teenagers. I don't recall the details, and we probably did a lot of things wrong. But when it got old enough to fend for itself, we removed a window screen and tearfully watched it go. We might as well have saved the drama—the bird kept coming back for a couple of years. It would greet us, sometimes fly into the house if a door was left open, and then out again, going about its business. I've saved a number of baby birds since then, but in my memory "Baby Birdy" is still the star.

There aren't many visible bugs on the island, though I'm sure bugs of various sorts exist by the million, even if they don't exactly come forward and introduce themselves. There are bumblebees, which I have to admit scare me a little, though

I've been told they're unlikely to sting. I loved some of the bugs in New Orleans—fireflies, which I've never seen anywhere else. Gorgeous butterflies. And dragonflies, locally called mosquito hawks. Those I've seen everywhere, but not like the New Orleans ones—gold, blue, green, and even copper-colored. I wonder if they're still there.

This month, we're going to look mostly at old cookie molds in garden themes—the antiques and also ones that have been produced recently but are no longer available. I'll give hints for how to find them and how to use them.

So there's lots of cookies to try. You can't garden all the time— you'd get sunburned. Isn't that a nice thought after the hard winter?

Tip: Where to Look for Old Cookie Molds

Cookie molds of various kinds have been made for centuries. The oldest, of course, are museum pieces. And until the twentieth century, most cookie molds were one-of-a-kind, handmade items. Most were hand carved from wood. Their popularity waned with the Industrial Revolution, when machine-made everything took the place of handcrafts and small artisans. Cookie molding itself went out of fashion.

Decades later, the craft was revived, primarily with manu-factured molds. Brown Bag Cookie Molds, which debuted in 1983, made pottery cookie molds and shortbread pans—the first mass-produced cookie molds I know of. One of their first molds was called Beautiful Swan.

In the next few years, many companies climbed on the bandwagon. An amazing array of pottery cookie molds, cookie stamps, and shortbread pans crowded the shelves of cookware shops and the pages of specialty catalogs.

Pottery molds have been overtaken by other materials. In 2006, Brown Bag produced their Swan Song mold as their last cookie mold, although they continue to make shortbread pans and cookie stamps. Most of their imitators have also stopped making molds.

But there are thousands and thousands of out-of-production cookie molds around. Some are antiques, others are just...used. You can find them on web sites such as Etsy and eBay—sometimes tagged as butter

molds, soap molds, or with other mistaken labels (and by the same token, not everything you see labeled as a cookie mold actually is one). There are often one or two in antique stores. Thrift stores often have a few, jumbled among mixed lots of used kitchenware. Some are underpriced, some are wildly overpriced. It's a treasure hunt.

As you look for old cookie molds, enjoy the journey! You may not find exactly the ones I found, but you're sure to find something good.

Tip: Using Antique Cookie Molds

The floral cookie pictured here comes from a very large, handmade, antique mold. Many old molds are very large—but if they're divided into several cookies, as this one is, there's no reason why you have to make all of them at once. You can press the dough into half the mold, or even make cookies one at a time.

The six small cookies shown are from a smaller mold, quite old. It's metal faced—I have wondered why there aren't more of these, because they're the only truly old ones where the design was mass-produced. This one is wood with a fairly thin, but very heavy, metal face. In addition to birds, this one features fishing, churning, a berry, and a home.

If you have an antique metal or metal-faced cookie mold, be aware that some of them are lead or pewter, an alloy that contains lead.

When you make multiple cookies with a mold, chill the formed dough well before cutting the cookies apart. Cut the cookies with a rolling cutter like a pastry wheel or pizza wheel.

Or if you use a knife, use an up and down, short chopping motion—don't drag it. If the dough sticks to the knife blade, flour the knife.

Separate the cookies from one another before baking, or they'll buckle as they bake.

Recipe: Soft Brandy Orange Cookies

Creaming soft butter and using mostly sugar for the sweetening produces a soft cookie. It may rise a little more in the oven and show the mold detail less sharply than a crisp honey cookie.

    1 cup (225 grams) unsalted butter
    1 large egg
    1 cup (200 grams) white sugar
    ⅛ teaspoon salt
    1 tablespoon milk or cream
    1 tablespoon honey
    1 tablespoon brandy extract
    1 teaspoon culinary orange oil
    ½ teaspoon orange extract
    About 4 cups (560 grams) all-purpose flour (plain flour)

    1. Preheat oven to 325°F (163°C)
    2. Cream the butter. Add the sugar gradually and continue creaming.
    3. Beat the egg in a large bowl until the yolk and white are fully mixed.

4. Add the beaten egg and salt to the butter mixture.

5. Mix the milk, honey, brandy extract, orange oil, and orange extract, and add to the egg mixture.

6. Add flour slowly and mix in until you have dough that is solid enough to knead.

7. Transfer the dough to a floured work surface. Continue adding flour by kneading in a little at a time until the dough is smooth and slightly sticky.

8. Roll and form the dough.

9. Bake for 15 to 20 minutes or until the edges have slightly browned and the top has begun to firm up.

Twentieth-Century Pottery Cookie Molds

Flowers, birds, and butterflies are popular motifs for twentieth century pottery molds, like this one from Brown Bag Cookie Molds. There are hundreds of other designs—designs for every holiday, every season and occasion, even for school teams, buildings, and states. The variety is amazing.

Many of these molds aren't produced anymore, but almost all are available if you keep your eyes open. I've found many beautiful pottery cookie molds in thrift shops, and of course, online auctions are a great place to look. Prices vary. Some out-of-production cookie molds are considered rare or collectible, so they're more expensive than similar ones that aren't unusual.

The cookies are nice when they're decorated, if you like to do that, but I don't think it's necessary. Most of the molds are so well designed that they're equally pretty without coloring. Occasionally, you'll find one that was designed for paper art rather than cookies—these may be shallower and less satisfactory for baking.

Shortbread pans were also made, but my experience with them has not been good. I don't recommend them for use in accordance with manufacturer's recommendations. You can get them to work as cookie molds if you use them for forming one cookie at a time and don't try to bake in them.

Recipe: Cinnamon Almond Cookies

These are fairly crisp, because they're made with melted butter. If you want a soft cookie, soften and cream the butter as I do in the recipe for Soft Brandy Orange Cookies.

1 cup (225 grams) unsalted butter
1 large egg
½ cup (100 grams) white sugar
½ cup firmly packed (100 grams) brown sugar
1 teaspoon cinnamon
⅛ teaspoon salt
1 tablespoon milk or cream
1 tablespoon molasses
2 teaspoons almond extract
½ teaspoon vanilla extract
About 4 cups (560 grams) all-purpose flour (plain flour)

1. Preheat oven to 325°F (163°C)

2. Melt the butter and set aside.

3. Beat the egg in a large bowl until the yolk and white are fully mixed.

4. Mix the white sugar, brown sugar, cinnamon, and salt and sift to remove lumps. Add to the egg. Beat until well mixed.

5. Mix the milk, molasses, almond extract, and vanilla extract, and add to the egg mixture.

6. Add the melted butter slowly and beat until well mixed. Don't just pour it in quickly—the heat still in the butter could cook the egg!

7. Add flour slowly and mix in until you have dough that is solid enough to knead.

8. Transfer the dough to a floured work surface. Continue adding flour by kneading in a little at a time until the dough is smooth and slightly sticky.

9. Roll and form the dough.

10. Bake for 15 to 20 minutes or until the edges have slightly browned and the top has begun to firm up.

Kashigata and Moon Cake Molds

Japanese sweets, called kashi, are made in these molds. They're not cookies, but the molds work well for cookies too. Kashigata molds may have a top layer, and they're likely to be more expensive if they do still have this piece. It's probably used for leveling the kashi, but I haven't found the upper piece useful in cookie molding.

The cookie shown is from an antique kashigata mold.

Chinese moon cakes, also quite different from western cookies, were the original inspiration for Brown Bag cookie molds. Moon cake molds are available in many designs, some very finely carved.

Metal Molds and Pans

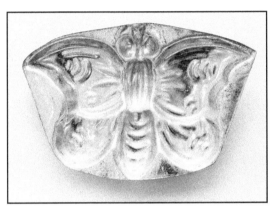

Metal molds and mold-like pans are available, in antique shops and elsewhere, but not all of them work well for cookies. Be careful to get one with sharp detailing—often pans are intended for chocolate molding, and aren't clear enough for cookies to look good, since they lose some detail when they bake.

Many metal molds and pans are too deep for cookies. I've had no luck at all in molding cookies in deep containers. Even if I use dough that I've rolled to a uniform thickness with rolling pin guides, the cookies come out lopsided. And retrieving the cookies from the bottom of a deep mold is nearly impossible.

But some pans do work. If a pan is well-detailed and no more than about ¼ inch deep, give it a try. Pans can be used to bake cookies in, or you can mold cookies with them and bake them on a sheet. You'll get different results, so compare and decide which you prefer.

With the softer cookies that are sweetened mostly with sugar, you may prefer baking in the mold. Sugar-sweetened cookies don't hold a pattern as well as honey cookies to begin with, so it makes a difference if they're baked in the mold. You may have to put nonstick foil and pie weights over large cookies to keep them from bubbling and heaving as they bake.

If you bake cookies in a thin metal mold, be careful—they burn very easily.

JUNE

June on the Island

When June comes to San Juan Island, we are more than ready for summer. But it is not always ready for us.

We pull summer clothes out of storage, but can't wear them yet. "Is it still this winter," I ask, "or has next winter come already?"

We joke about June-uary, but we wish it would warm up just a little. Everything is flowering now, especially the dandelions and California poppies, but we still wear jackets when we go out, even during the daytime. True, in a few weeks we will be grumbling that it's just so *hot*, but it's hard to imagine that now. It seems as if summer will never come.

Wedding announcements appear in the island newspapers, and probably the brides and grooms are more comfortable in their finery than if the weather here were hot. The cakes stand intact, I suppose, with no threat of the icing melting during the toasts.

I've been to large weddings—and was very impressed by the level of celebration, not to mention the organization that went into them. And I've been to more than a few small ones, including my own. The picture at the head of this page is a treasured photo of mine—my own bouquet, picked the morning of my wedding by a friend with a garden. Since there were only two guests—our witnesses—there was no one to throw the bouquet at, so I kept it. Put it in a glass that I bought for my first apartment when I was nineteen years old, and photographed it before Aaron and I left for our Catalina honeymoon.

Large or small, weddings are among the most memorable days in a person's life. Everything seems to need to be special.

Can you really make molded cookies for a wedding? You can get beautiful molds, but do you have the time and energy to do this? I've made refreshments for a few friends' weddings, and I know it's something you make time for. But—and here's the big consideration—you don't have time and energy to spend on something that may not work, or that may turn out to be a lot more effort than you'd counted on.

So this month, I offer a couple of recipes I consider to be about as no-fail as a recipe can possibly be. One is a cookie recipe that includes apple jelly in the ingredients—this makes a particularly easy dough because some of the jelly ingredients are dough stabilizers. Perfect if you want to make important cookies, like cookies for a wedding party, but you haven't done it before.

Cake Topper Molds

Cake topper molds are a beautiful way to decorate cakes with fondant or marzipan. Coincidentally, at least some of the cake topper molds — like these from House on the

Hill—also make wonderful cookies. The large cookies make great gifts especially when you back them with a cake board (more or less like the cardboard round a pizza comes on) and wrap with shrink wrap.

Tip: More on Marzipan

Marzipan is a lot like cookie dough—except you're not going to bake it. And, instead of preventing sticking with flour, as you do with dough, you'll use sifted powdered sugar.

If you buy marzipan ready made, which I advise, let a chunk of it come to room temperature and knead it to make it flexible. Use powdered sugar on your kneading surface and on your hands so it won't be sticky.

Then simply press it into your mold, which you've also dusted with powdered sugar. It should be easy to peel the mold off it once you have it pressed in enough to get a clean image.

Trim the edges, and you're done!

To make a thin sheet of marzipan, roll the kneaded marzipan out to the thickness you want. For thinner sheets, you may want to use rolling guides—either "perfection strips," which you lay alongside the dough to control the thickness, or rolling pin rings that fit over the ends.

When you have a flat sheet of the thickness you want, brush powdered sugar on top. Press the mold down into the marzipan firmly to get a clear impression. Then peel the mold off gently and trim the marzipan to the shapes you want.

To stick the marzipan pieces to your cookies, use cake frosting.

For my earlier tips on marzipan and a recipe, see the February section of this book.

Recipe: Easy Wedding Cookies

These cookies unmold easily and bake without losing detail.

1 cup (225 grams) unsalted butter
1 large egg
⅔ cup (160 milliliters) apple jelly
1 teaspoon vanilla extract
¼ teaspoon natural lemon flavoring
⅔ cup (135 grams) sugar
¼ teaspoon salt
About 5 cups (700 grams) all-purpose flour (plain flour)

1. Melt the butter and set aside.

2. Beat the egg in a large bowl until yolk and white are fully mixed.

3. Mix the jelly, vanilla extract, and lemon flavoring. Add to the egg and beat until well mixed.

4. Mix the sugar and salt. Add to the egg mixture and beat until well mixed.

5. Add the melted butter slowly and beat until well mixed.

6. Add flour slowly until the dough is solid enough to knead.

7. Knead in additional flour until the dough is the consistency of children's modeling clay.

8. Roll the cookie dough to a uniform thickness. Mold per the instructions at the beginning of this book.

9. Bake the cookies at 325°F (163°C) for ten to twelve minutes.

Tip: Flavoring Extracts and Waters

Flavoring extracts work well in molded cookies, because you get strong flavor without adding texture or much color or liquid.

But you have to be careful.

One of the most important things to remember is, avoid artificial flavors if natural ones are available. Artificial vanilla flavor, for example, is much less expensive than natural, but the flavors aren't nearly the same. That's true of lemon, as well, and many others.

Another thing to be careful about is whether the flavoring is a familiar one. It's nice to use a little rose water or orange flower water in wedding cookies—but don't go overboard. Balance them with other natural flavorings that are more familiar. If you don't, the cookies may remind people of inedible substances like shampoo.

Wedding Cookie Molds

Here are a few wonderful choices for wedding cookies.

The Wedding Coach

The wedding coach is a centuries-old tradition, and an elegant image for a cookie mold, though few of us are likely to actually ride in one. But for a reception, wouldn't this design be perfect and unique?

The Bridal Arch

Here's a beautiful cookie with symbols of the bride and groom and the vows they exchange. It's a springerle mold, which means you mold the cookie first, then cut it out. If you have only round cookie cutters, you can still cut an oval—see directions in the April section of this book.

Wedding Cookie Stamps

Inexpensive and easy to use, cookie stamps with traditional wedding themes may be just what you need. This one's from Rykraft.

Heart Cookie Tartlets

These cookies can be filled with a little dab of buttercream frosting, lemon curd, or flavored soft cream cheese.

JULY

Picnics in July

If San Juan Island is ever going to have hot weather, July is the time. Suddenly, we go from our usual complaining about the cold to either enjoying the heat or griping about it. I'm one of the gripers, I'm afraid. I don't mind heat—since I grew up in New Orleans, summers on the island don't actually seem all that hot. But it's so still here on hot days. The expression, "The wind has died," seems all too literal. The wind seems to be actually dead, as if we'll never feel it again.

Fans hum all day and all night, and opening or closing particular windows becomes a major decision. The ones that open onto the cool spot under the cherry tree? Yes, let's open those. The larger ones at the south-facing deck? Maybe not. Moving from one chair to another requires a major effort.

Still, summer is just glorious. Flowers are everywhere. Swaths of bright blossoms, with a bright blue sea shining in the distance, are a sort of Friday Harbor signature. Sailboats, too—though my enthusiasm for sailing has been curtailed by knowing how cold the water is, even in July. Aaron and I took a few sailing lessons when we lived in Olympia, and one of the first things the instructor did was to warn us how short a time you can survive in the water of Puget Sound before you die of hypothermia. Since I originally learned to sail in Florida, this got my attention all too well, and I abandoned the idea of northern sailing. Still, the boats are lovely to watch.

The town of Friday Harbor goes all out for the Fourth of July weekend. It's the height of the tourist season, and the streets and shops are jammed. Everyone is having a good time. There's a picnic to celebrate the Pig War, which is among the interesting trivia of U.S. history. Here's the story:

In 1856, the border between Canada and the United States was marked off by the Treaty of Oregon. Unfortunately, the treaty had its vague spots, and a major one was setting the local part of the border in "the middle of the Channel which separates the continent from Vancouver Island." Sounds fine, but there are *two* major channels, one on either side of the San Juan Islands. Naturally, the British, who governed Canada at that time, interpreted the treaty as giving them the islands, while the United States saw it the other way.

In 1859, nationals from both countries lived in the islands. The "war" was started when an American farmer shot a pig belonging to a British citizen. This precipitated a military standoff that lasted until 1872, when the territorial dispute was settled by arbitration. The pig was actually the only casualty.

We still have two parks: "English Camp" and "American Camp" at opposite ends of the island, located where the garrisons were— and still with a few historic buildings left from them. The two sites together are now a National Historic Park, the only one in the United States to celebrate the peaceful settlement of a dispute.

The pig's name—if it had one—has not come down to us in the historical account. But I was able to find a pig cookie mold to celebrate its role in our history.

So, on with the summer picnics! This month's cookies are "picnic cookies," meaning they're rather small and not too delicate.

This means more honey cookies, which are less likely to end up as crumbs at the bottom of the picnic basket. Then, too, a picnic seems a good opportunity for sandwich cookies. You can put in some fancy flavors in the lower layer of the sandwich and the filling. Pack your picnic basket and set off for a beautiful afternoon. Look out for ants!

Recipe: Creamy Coconut Cookies

This is a favorite I'm repeating from *Baking with Cookie Molds*. Cream of coconut takes the place of honey in this recipe. It's a syrup, so it has the same effect.

½ cup (115 grams) unsalted butter
1 large egg
1 cup (235 milliliters) canned cream of coconut (See notes.)
1 tablespoon coconut extract
½ teaspoon vanilla
½ cup (100 grams) sugar
1 teaspoon vanilla
¼ teaspoon salt
About 4½ cups (630 grams) all-purpose flour (plain flour)

1. Melt the butter and set aside.
2. Beat the egg in a large bowl until yolk and white are fully mixed.
3. Mix the cream of coconut, coconut extract, and vanilla extract. Add to the egg and beat until well mixed.
4. Mix the sugar and salt. Add to the egg mixture and beat until well mixed.
5. Add the melted butter slowly and beat until well mixed.
6. Add flour slowly until the mixture is solid enough to knead.
7. Transfer to your work surface and knead in more flour to make a soft, slightly sticky dough.
8. Wrap or cover the dough and refrigerate for up to ½ hour—until it's firm but still flexible.
9. Roll and form the dough.

10. Refrigerate the cookies while you preheat the oven to 350°F (175°C), or lower for especially thick cookies.

11. Bake for 10 to 15 minutes or until the edges have slightly browned and the top has begun to firm up.

Notes

Cream of coconut is a sweetened mixture used in drinks and desserts. It is not to be confused with coconut cream, which is unsweetened. Like natural peanut butter, cream of coconut tends to separate, so stir to blend well before measuring.

Modern Makers and Their Molds

In May, we looked at antique cookie molds. Most of them were made by carvers who didn't sign their work. Their names are lost today, although their carvings remain. Sometimes I look at an old cookie mold and wonder about the person who made it— and all the people who have used it over the years.

Cookie molds are still being carved, although some of the ones you'll find are unsigned. Other carvers are deservedly well known, and some are masters. There will be no lack of handmade wooden cookie molds from our era to bequeath to the future—a pleasing thought. History is about many things, and only a few— usually unpleasant things like border disputes—make it into the history books. I like to think of a history of fall afternoons, a carver quietly making a plank of cherry into a treasure, a baker turning out fine cookies for a party.

In addition to molds for picnic cookies, we're looking at modern cookie mold makers this month. Some of them are carvers; others use newer materials. Here I've featured ones whose work I'm personally familiar with.

Modern Wood Molds

Wood is the oldest tradition, of course. Wood cookie molds go back for centuries, and many can only be seen now in museums. However, various approaches, including hand carving, machine carving, and laser carving, live on in the hands of some skilled modern cookie mold artists.

Gene Wilson, HOBI Cookie Molds

My very first cookie mold was a St. Nicholas mold carved by Gene Wilson. Maybe that was why I fell in love with cookie molds.

Gene has been carving molds since 1972. According to his web site: "Gene has worked to perfect his technique of power tool engraving with a hand-held router. This innovative, self-taught type of freehand carving has allowed a vast variety of molds to be offered at affordable prices. Since no carving templates are used, each mold is an original carving with it's own 'personality.'"

The molds I've bought from Gene have all been cherry, but he also works in beech.

Vince Marine

Vince makes custom cookie molds, and has also made molds for House on the Hill.

Vince lives and works in suburban Chicago where he carves cookie molds in his home studio. What makes his molds special is the sculptural quality, depth, and high degree of detail.

Dan and Jane Coultis, Cherry Cookie Molds

According to the Cherry Cookie Molds web site, Dan and Jane Coultis were inspired to create "...molds that are more of an American style…, something that was new, fresh and would resonate with Americans."

The products are made of hardwood and machined using traditional and advanced woodworking machinery. The wood supplied currently is sourced from the mountains of Eastern Tennessee.

Kyna Campbell, My Cookie Mold

Campbell's molds are laser cut, and highly detailed.

Because of the fine detail, I prefer to prepare these molds with a light dusting of flour, no oil. I get a better print, and the cookies release better.

Jan VandeVoorde

I've never made a cookie with this mold, partly because it's too big for my cookie sheet or my oven.

The mold's unique images did inspire me to write a story, "Journey to the Twelfth Night Market," which you'll find in the January section of this book. I'm sure the plot I came up with was far from what Mr. VandeVoorde had in mind when he carved the mold, but it made sense to me.

If your oven is larger than mine, and if you have a large mold, the December section has helpful tips for handling large cookies.

Mr. VandeVoorde lives in Belgium, and is regarded as a modern master carver.

Walter Geluyckens

Walter Geluyckens is considered another of the modern masters of cookie mold carving.

I don't own one of his molds, but this photo of one of his beautiful carvings was supplied by a friend.

S. R. White Carving

The mold shown, called a "double thistle" mold in White's catalog, is one of several thistle motif molds made by the company. Their molds are detailed but release the dough well, which makes them especially suitable for beginners.

Composition Molds

Composition molds may or may not be treasured by collectors, the way the historic wooden molds are. But the modern ones are the reliable workhorses of today's cookie molders.

They often reproduce historic wooden molds that we could only sigh over in museums, if these beauties hadn't been replicated for general use.

In addition, composition molds are easier to use than almost any other type of mold. They have very little tendency to stick to the dough. They are also easy to clean and store.

Older composition molds, such as those made by the Laxa Family, are decorative, and are not considered food safe. Molds from the following artists are for food use:

The Springerle Baker

The Springerle Baker makes molds of all sizes. This is a cookie from one of their smaller molds—it would be perfect for a picnic cookie, and adaptable as a sandwich cookie as well.

Their web site offers classes, recipes, and instructions for using the molds for crafts.

Springerle Joy

Springerle Joy makes a wide variety of composition molds. This is one of their smaller geometric molds—it would make a good picnic or sandwich cookie.

Their web site offers videos, classes, and recipes as well as molds.

House on the Hill

Originally a direct supplier, House on the Hill has converted their business to strictly wholesale. This mold by House on the Hill is perfect for picnic cookies. It's even called Fireworks!

Pottery Molds

Pottery molds are not traditional like wood, but they're still very nice for molding and collecting.

Brown Bag Cookie Molds

First, the pig! Celebrated in our island's Pig War festivities—this would be a perfect cookie for the local picnic. The pig that started it all. How could a cute guy like this start so much trouble?

Most of the Brown Bag molds, including this one, are no longer produced, but they're easy to find used. They do continue to sell shortbread pans and cookie stamps.

Zanda Panda

This company makes stoneware molds in original designs. Various kinds and sizes. The one shown here is one of their smaller designs, ideal for picnic or sandwich cookies

JBK Pottery

This manufacturer makes cookie stamps in a variety of designs.

Other Manufacturers

Molds were made (or distributed) by Hartstone, Pampered Chef, Cotton Press, Hermitage, Longaberger, Pfaltzgraff, and others. Many of these molds are available in online sales and auctions, but as far as I know, none of the manufacturers are still making cookie molds.

Silicone Molds

And now for something really nontraditional!

Zanda Panda

In addition to the stoneware cookie molds shown in the preceding article, Zanda Panda makes a limited number of silicone shortbread pans. These are actually the only bake-in-the-mold shortbread pans I've had good results with.

Recipe: Maple Orange Cookies

These make great sandwich cookies with fig preserves as a filling.

> 1 cup (225 grams) unsalted butter
> 1 large egg
> ½ cup (160 milliliters) maple syrup
> 1 teaspoon natural orange extract
> ½ teaspoon culinary orange oil
> ½ teaspoon maple flavoring extract
> ¼ cup (50 grams) sugar
> ¼ cup (37 grams) maple sugar
> ½ teaspoon cinnamon
> ¼ teaspoon salt
> About 4¾ cups (665 grams) all-purpose flour (plain flour)

1. Melt the butter and set aside.

2. Beat the egg in a large bowl until yolk and white are fully mixed.

3. Mix the maple syrup, orange extract, orange oil, and lemon flavoring. Add to the egg and beat until well mixed.

4. Mix the sugars, cinnamon, and salt. Add to the egg mixture and beat until well mixed.

5. Add the melted butter slowly and beat until well mixed.

6. Add flour slowly until the dough is solid enough to knead.

7. Knead in additional flour until the dough is the consistency of children's modeling clay.

8. Roll the cookie dough to a uniform thickness. Mold per the instructions for your cookie molds.

9. Bake the cookies at 325°F (163°C) for ten to twelve minutes.

AUGUST

The Island in August

Finally, for however short a moment, it's summer on San Juan Island. Compared to the rest of the country, our summer is mild. No doubt that's why this is our visitor season. I think they come not only for the sweet weather, but also for the island scenery and for the "island time" phenomenon, a relaxed atmosphere that's harder and harder to find these days. It's a very low-pressure sort of place. More than once, I've offered my spot in line at the grocery store to someone who had just one or two items, only to have them thank me and refuse, saying they're in no hurry.

We'll have a short dry spell between now and Labor Day, probably. The grass will turn brown, and any flowers worth saving will have to be watered daily. Of course, the weeds will still thrive! However, at least half the weeds are California poppies. They're bright and cheerful, and really, people in other places plant and tend them. So maybe I should call them wildflowers. This year I'll try to just enjoy it all.

Last year, I got what I thought was a genius idea. I bought fancy California poppies from a seed company, red, white, ruffled, double and every possible variation. I planted and watered them—and every last plant blossomed with ordinary orange flowers. I give up.

A doe visits our back yard frequently, but she's camera-shy, so I don't have pictures. She doesn't seem to be eating anything—not that there's anything back there a deer would like—just checking us out. I'd guess her objective is the neighbors' lovingly-tended lettuce. If so, their life probably isn't quite as low-stress as mine.

As August ends, we have the County Fair, our goodbye to summer. I've never entered my molded cookies in the baking event. I don't like competition, even when I win. I go and look at the cookies, though, and wish someone else would make molded cookies for the islanders to see. Maybe someday. A couple of island stores are selling my first cookie molds book now. Maybe the idea will catch on.

This August section features cookies and cookie projects for children, with an emphasis on younger kids, since older ones can use cookie molds in the same ways as adults. We'll look at designs that appeal to kids, from cartoon characters to a triceratops. Also a few cookie molds that feature children, and two hornbook molds—those alphabet slates that were supposed to help kids learn to read. And even homemade animal crackers!

And, of course, recipes!

Tip: Kid-Friendly Cookie Molds

Kid-themed cookie molds, like this one from Cotton Press, are sometimes the same as molds made for grown-ups. Not always, though. And some of them are disappointing. Here's what you need to know:

1. Standard cavity molds such as many Brown Bag molds or carved wood molds are difficult for very young children to use. If a parent helps, the task of getting the cookie out of the

mold should be done by the adult. Older kids and teens probably won't have trouble with any cookie mold.

2. Cookie stamps are especially kid-friendly. If you pair them with cookie cutters, they're especially easy.

3. Some inexpensive kid-themed cookie molds work better for candy than for cookies. The cookies they make will be disappointingly blurry unless you paint the cookies to bring the patterns out. You can paint cookies with decorating gel or with light corn syrup with added food colors.

4. Some plastic and silicone molds are great for kids, and they're inexpensive and unbreakable, too.

5. Any of these molds will work with any of my recipes. If younger kids are doing the project, it's probably best to choose simpler recipes that don't require a lot of detailed attention or especially careful handling.

Tip: Kids and Flavors

Kids' flavor preferences tend to be different from those of adults. Of course, there are exceptions to every rule, but there are trends.

Most children like simpler, sweeter flavors. They haven't developed a tolerance for sharp or bitter flavors yet, if they ever will.

Most don't like exotic flavors. They like mild fruit flavors, and many like chocolate—but not strong, bitter chocolate or mocha.

When making cookies for kids, I'd be careful with spices, if they're in the recipe. If I'm making gingerbread for adults, for example, I'd always use fresh ginger—many adults love the hot, pungent taste. For kids, I'd use the milder ground ginger from my spice rack.

Recipe: Your Own Animal Cookies

Packaged animal cookies are appealing mostly because of their shapes. They're rather dry, plain cookies with a faint lemon flavor. You can do much better with the recipe below. Then use animal molds such as this delightful rolling pin from House on the Hill.

When you use a patterned rolling pin, put your dough on a table that's low enough that you're pushing down rather than out. Counters are too high for this, at least for most of us.

Small children would need help in using a rolling pin like this, but older kids should be able to have a lot of fun with it. Rolling pins are one of the quickest and easiest ways to make molded cookies.

    1 cup (225 grams) unsalted butter
    1 large egg
    ½ cup (120 milliliters) honey
    ½ teaspoon natural lemon flavoring
    ½ cup (100 grams) sugar
    ⅛ teaspoon salt
    ½ cup (46 grams) finely ground oat flour
    About 4 cups (560 grams) all-purpose flour (plain flour)

1. Melt the butter and set aside.

2. Beat the egg in a large bowl until the yolk and white are fully mixed.

3. Mix the honey and lemon flavoring. Add to the egg and beat until well mixed.

4. Mix the sugar and salt. Add to the egg mixture and beat until well mixed.

5. Add the melted butter slowly and beat until well mixed. Don't just pour it in quickly—the heat still in the butter could cook the egg!

6. Mix the oat flour with about half the all-purpose flour (plain flour).

7. Add the oat flour mixture to the cookie dough.

8. Transfer the dough to a floured work surface. Continue adding all-purpose flour (plain flour) by kneading in a little at a time until the dough is smooth and slightly sticky.

9. Wrap or cover the dough to prevent drying, then refrigerate to make it less sticky. This should take half an hour at most.

10. Roll and form the dough.

11. Refrigerate the cookies while you preheat the oven to 350°F (175°C)

12. Bake for 10 to 15 minutes or until the edges have slightly browned.

Plastic Animal Molds

Plastic molds, usually in sheets with several designs, are widely available in craft and cooking stores. Here we have an inexpensive plastic mold with cheerful animal pictures from Wilton. The manufacturer's label photo shows detailed, charming animals in multiple colors.

Here's what you need to watch out for when you're buying cookie molds of this kind, though: the label picture shows very shiny animals, almost certainly candy. It's much easier to make a molded shape with candy, which sets in the mold, than with a cookie, because the cookie blurs as it's baked.

I think this mold is delightful for molding candy, but is much less effective for cookies. But it's certainly not fragile, and kids might have fun with it.

Gingerbread Kids Molds

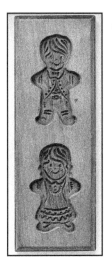

There are gingerbread men and gingerbread women. Gene Wilson of HOBI Cookie Molds also offers this mold for gingerbread kids.

Of course you can use this for cookies other than gingerbread. It's easier to make the cookies one at a time rather than try to make both at once.

Probably younger children would need help unmolding the cookies. Anyone could have lots of fun decorating them. The mold makes a nice, sharp impression.

Recipe: Gingerbread for Kids

This is a simpler, milder gingerbread than I'd make for adults. It's also a soft cookie, not crisp like gingersnaps.

If your kids enjoy spicy foods, you can increase all the spices—up to doubling.

1 cup (225 grams) unsalted butter
1 large egg
1 cup (200 grams) white sugar
⅛ teaspoon salt
1 tablespoon milk or cream
1 tablespoon molasses
1 teaspoon cinnamon
1 teaspoon ground ginger
½ teaspoon allspice
About 4 cups (560 grams) all-purpose flour (plain flour)

1. Cream the butter. Add the sugar gradually and continue creaming.

2. Beat the egg in a large bowl until the yolk and white are fully mixed.

3. Add the beaten egg and salt to the butter mixture.

4. Mix the milk, honey, ginger, and cinnamon, and add to the egg mixture.

6. Add flour slowly and mix in until you have dough that is solid enough to knead.

7. Transfer the dough to a floured work surface. Continue adding flour by kneading in a little at a time until the dough is smooth and slightly sticky.

8. Roll and form the dough.

9. Bake for 15 to 20 minutes or until the edges have slightly browned and the top has begun to firm up.

Horse Molds

How I longed for a horse when I was a little girl! There was the side issue that I was terrified of them—that would probably have been a problem. And my parents weren't about to add horse care to the family budget.

So I settled for horse books. It was similar to being an armchair traveler—I was an armchair rider.

I think many children admire horses, and here's a cookie mold from House on the Hill that's perfect for them. Unbreakable, and easy to use since it's a springerle mold that works like a rubber stamp.

Almost any horse-crazy kid would love a horse cookie mold.

Tip: Favorite Cartoon Characters

Kids enjoy making cookies in the shapes of their favorite characters, but be aware that use of these molds is restricted. Images of cartoon characters are copyrighted, so you can only use them for making cookies for personal use. If you're selling cookies, some copyright holders have been known to object legally to the use of their images, even if sales are in small local venues such as farmers' markets.

Hornbook Molds

What is a hornbook, exactly? It's a device for teaching children to read. They were used in the days before printed books were common.

The first mold shown is from Springerle Joy. You see how the reversed letters in the mold print normally in the cookie.

Next is a small hornbook mold from The Springerle Baker.

"School days, school days..." That's probably the last thing kids want to think about at this point! But these hornbook molds are interesting. There's a story that the cookies would be a reward for the child learning the alphabet, but I doubt it. Still, it's a nice thought.

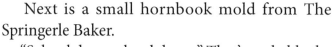

These molds are so interesting, in fact, that carver Gene Wilson has a page dedicated to hornbooks, their history, and cookie molds in the shape of hornbooks. The last hornbook mold is his.

More Molds for Kids

Here are a few more kinds of mold that kids are likely to enjoy.

Cookie Stamps

Brown Bag Cookie Molds makes quite a few charming, toy-like stamps, like this one of a tea party. Though they're fancy, the handles and little ornaments are made of resin, and seem sturdy. Their design would make them especially fun for kids to use.

Cookie stamps are used in much the same way as a rubber stamp. Stamp the dough, cut the cookie out with a cookie cutter, then remove the excess dough before stamping the next cookie.

Elves

I definitely believed in fairies and elves when I was little. Maybe this was because my family was of Irish extraction, or maybe because we were literary as well. But I had wonderful books about fairies, and they were on about the same level for me as horse books—adventures in something that was real, just not part of my day to day existence.

I made fairy dresses out of rose petals. Even I could see that they fell far short of the dresses fairies wore in my books, but I comforted myself that no doubt the fairies could improve them with magic. I'm not sure why it didn't occur to me that they might just as well have made the dresses by magic with no help from me. I was well-intentioned, just a little illogical.

This cookie mold is from Springerle Joy.

Dinosaurs

Dinosaurs are popular with kids—at least they were with my nephews. Several kinds of them have been used as models for cookie molds. These might be fun for kids to paint and decorate, too.

This one is a triceratops. It was one of a group of dinosaur molds made by Brown Bag. The group also included a stegosaurus and a T. Rex.

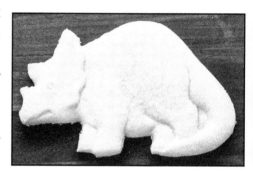

Dogs

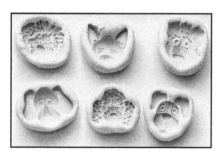

Here's another fun set I found online. Small silicone molds that make pictures of dog faces. These would be ideal for small children.

I tried them with rolled dough, but the results weren't good. Finally, I tried making one-inch balls of dough, and pressing the little molds into them. This worked much better.

You can find all kinds of kid-friendly molds by searching the Internet for "silicone cookie molds." Happy hunting, and happy baking!

SEPTEMBER

September on the Island

September brings big changes to San Juan Island. All summer, the island has been like a party, a vacation. We look around at unfamiliar faces, realizing that people work hard all year for the privilege of spending two weeks in a place we live in. We take the island less for granted now. True, it has its drawbacks—the isolation, the lack of choice. But it's a beautiful, safe, friendly place. We remember why we came here.

Slowly, like migrating birds, the visitors go home. Back to their schools, their jobs, their comparatively warm winters in the Southwest—or their colder ones in New York or Chicago. The afternoon light looks golden at this time of year. The days are still long, but we know winter is around the corner.

Still a few days to sit on the lawn with a view of the bay. Still a few excursions around the island, maybe a ferry trip to another island just for the fun of it. Late summer and early fall are the time to wash quilts, or anything else that must dry in the sun, because it's our only reliable dry season. Soon the summer clothes will be packed away, the coats and boots will come out of hiding. We're on a steep hill, so the lightest snowfall can strand us if there's any ice on the road. We lay in winter supplies—canned goods, drinking water, milk in boxes. We are like squirrels—except that the island has no squirrels. When spring comes, we'll donate any of our unused hoard to the food bank.

We make sure our emergency lanterns are charged—Fall brings wild windstorms here. The power company is good about repairing outages, but you do need light in the interval.

Saying goodbye to summer and preparing for the coming cold and dark—that's September. But we love the island in all seasons, and feel a little sorry for our visitors, because they never get to see it on a wild winter night. They have their memories and their photographs of blue sea and flowers, but they haven't heard the wind rushing through the cedars like a freight train or seen a mist of frost, sparkling like dancing sugar, swirling above the road to the beach.

Every season has its delights, and if you're a quilter, fall begins a time of planning and creating quilts! Even on San Juan Island, summer days can be too hot for quilting in your lap, even if you use a frame. Fall brings new possibilities, and new reasons to make quilts.

Gifts, maybe for the holidays, if you work quickly or your project is small. Keeping you or your loved ones warm in the cold, windy island winters. Even just something to do when it's too cold to go out.

The quilt shown here was made by my great-grandmother. It may have been made together with friends—some of the embroidery that decorates it suggests that it's a friendship quilt.

Quilt Cookie Molds

There are many cookie molds in quilt patterns, and the cookies just beg to be decorated. This delightful design by Louise Sturdivant, from a mold by Cotton Press, reminds me of quilted wall hangings, complete with fabric patterns! You might not want to do something this special very often, but even a simpler decorating job will look charming.

Especially if you plan to paint the cookies, you'll want a recipe with a light colored dough. It should also be very fine-textured, so you won't have lumps and bumps.

This is probably not the best use for layer cookies, because the lower-layer goodies can make the surface slightly irregular.

Recipe: Quilters' Tea Cookies

I've always enjoyed orange spice tea, so this cookie recipe is based on those flavors.

>   1 cup (225 grams) unsalted butter
>   1 large egg
>   ½ cup (120 milliliters) honey
>   1 tablespoon freshly squeezed orange juice
>   1 teaspoon natural orange flavoring
>   ½ teaspoon culinary orange oil

⅛ teaspoon natural lemon flavoring
½ cup (100 grams) sugar
1 teaspoon finely ground cinnamon
¼ teaspoon ground cloves
⅛ teaspoon salt
About 4½ cups (630 grams) all-purpose flour (plain
    flour)

1. Melt the butter and set aside.

2. Beat the egg in a large bowl until the yolk and white are fully mixed.

3. Mix the honey, orange juice, orange flavoring, orange oil, and lemon flavoring. Add to the egg and beat until well mixed.

4. Mix the sugar, cinnamon, cloves, and salt. Add to the egg mixture and beat until well mixed. If the mixture isn't smooth, don't worry—it will become smooth as you add the flour.

5. Add the melted butter slowly and beat until well mixed. Don't just pour it in quickly—the heat still in the butter could cook the egg!

6. Add flour slowly and mix in until you have dough that is solid enough to knead.

7. Transfer the dough to a floured work surface. Continue adding flour by kneading in a little at a time until the dough is smooth and slightly sticky.

8. Wrap or cover the dough to prevent drying, then refrigerate to make it less sticky. This should take half an hour at most.

9. Roll and form the dough.

10. Refrigerate the cookies while you preheat the oven to 350°F (175°C).

11. Bake for 10 to 15 minutes or until the edges have slightly browned and the top has begun to firm up.

More Quilt Cookie Molds

Here are more cookies and molds from quilt patterns and motifs.

Heart in Hand

Here's the heart motif again, superimposed on a hand this time in a mold from Brown Bag Cookie Molds. This may have originally been a love token, but a similar motif was also used by the Shakers to mean "Hands to work, hearts to God."

Schoolhouse Quilt

More quilt-themed cookies from Louise Sturdivant! Here we see two different painting treatments of cookies from the same mold. The flowers, bright colors, and azure background of the first cookie are like a colorful village on the seaside. The strong colors of the second cookie are perfect for the bright flowers she uses in the border.

These were made with a Brown Bag mold called Schoolhouse Quilt. It's actually for paper molding, which calls for a much shallower mold. Without the painting, then, the cookie would not be nearly as effective. Like almost all Brown Bag molds, it's no longer available new. It isn't difficult to find a used one, though, and it shouldn't be expensive.

Tulip Basket

The mold for this cookie comes from Cotton Press. I like the way the stitching is detailed in the mold itself. A square shape quilt block that is placed diagonally is said to be "on point."

Baltimore Album

Baltimore Album quilts are a distinctive and very beautiful style. The designs go back at least to the mid-nineteenth century. Traditional colors include bright reds and greens on a white background. Many of the motifs are floral. The style is still popular with quilters today.

This cookie, from a Cotton Press mold, shows a very simple Baltimore Album block, and Louise Sturdivant has painted it in traditional colors. Note the stitching of the quilting lines, carefully picked out against the natural cookie color. Louise has chosen a light background to duplicate the usual color of the Baltimore Album quilts.

Homespun Heart

This mold was made by Pampered Chef, and is now out of production, but easy to find used, and inexpensive. I don't know of a quilt block with all these elements, but the star element is a traditional one called "Ohio Star." Painting by Louise Sturdivant.

Vase of Flowers

This is one in the Pfaltzgraff "America" series, no longer made but still easily available. It's a motif that's found in both decorative painting and appliquéed quilts.

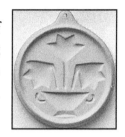

Pine Tree

This mold is another in the Pfaltzgraff "America" series. Pine Tree is a traditional patchwork pattern, almost always produced as a rectangular block. So the round cookie mold uses its decorative elements while re-interpreting the design.

A Cookie Quilt

Finale: a whole quilt!

Imagine how cute it would look to arrange a tray of cookies to make a whole quilt! Here's one you might make for a baby shower, but the possibilities are endless! Tip: have the background color match the color of the cookie edge so minor irregularities will disappear.

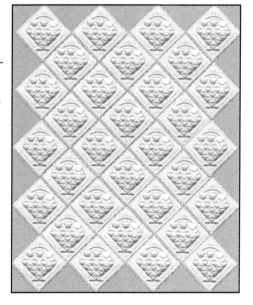

OCTOBER

Halloween

From ghoulies and ghosties
And long-leggedy beasties,
And things that go bump in the night,
Good Lord, deliver us!

—Traditional Scottish prayer

Halloween is an odd time. We revel in our fears, or in symbols of them. Just for one night, we impersonate the things we dread most.

Or maybe not. I remember one Halloween when my sister and I— aged about seven and five, respectively—dressed up as flowers. Day-Glo tulips, hot pink and orange— which may or may not be scary, depending on your point of view. Cartoon characters, pets, and superheroes seem to have a lot of adherents in the children I've seen recently. Friday Harbor has a Halloween parade, and the kids march up Spring Street in their costumes. It's fun for everyone. Most of the costumes don't seem too scary.

Just the same, Halloween has not lost its dark side. There are still images of a harvest moon rising above a ramshackle Victorian house, of witches riding brooms, and ghosts appearing in the cemetery. Pressed to define a witch, I doubt if I could have produced much besides a description of a crabby old lady in black clothes. Well, I'm an old lady myself now, and I have my crabby moments. And I wear black quite often, mostly because my husband likes me to. It sets off my silver hair.

My one effort at truly impersonating a witch resulted in a rather narrow escape. One year when I had a job in a recreation program, we were instructed to wear a costume to work and—with my black wardrobe—the choice was easy. All I needed was a pointed hat, which I acquired, and successfully impersonated a witch all day at work. Halloween being the last day of the month, it was payday, and we duly received our checks. And I didn't go to the bank after work, because I was just too tired.

Good thing—that branch had been held up earlier in the afternoon by a woman dressed as a witch. Heaven only knows how I would have been received if I'd strolled in there in my witch outfit. With a SWAT team, probably.

Here's my October wish for you: May your ghoulies and ghosties and long-leggedy beasties all be cookies!

Halloween Cookie Molds

Many Halloween cookie molds are available, but they aren't antique designs, as far as I've seen. Although Halloween goes back in history to ancient Celtic times, it wasn't celebrated by baking. Halloween cookie cutters have been around for a while, but the molds are relatively recent. They may coincide with the change in ways of celebrating the holiday, with trick-or-treating being replaced by private parties.

So check current cookie mold vendors to see what they offer. Cats, bats, hats, and spiders—they're likely to have something for just about any Halloween theme you can think of. There are lots of ghosts, haunted houses, witches, and other scary things as well.

Here are a few of my favorites.

Witch

This Brown Bag witch is really rather sweet-looking, as witches go. I'm not sure why the cat has fluffed his fur—maybe he doesn't like brooms.

Cat

Not very fierce-looking, is he? The fur is fluffed, but the face doesn't look at all evil. Still, he's definitely a Halloween cat. The mold is from Brown Bag.

Haunted House

This Wilton mold only needs a few ghosts to prove it's haunted! Or maybe it has ghosts, only they're the kind you don't exactly see.

Pumpkin

You can also get jack-o'-lantern molds from some vendors. With this plain pumpkin, though, you can use it again at Thanksgiving. Perfect for the Pumpkin Pecan Cheesecake Cookie recipe in *Baking with Cookie Molds*! Or any pumpkin molded cookie recipe. I'm sure it would be cute painted, too. The mold is from Brown Bag.

Three from Zanda Panda

A bat, a cat, and a witch! These would be great for your Halloween party!

Recipe: Chocolate Chip
Layer Cookies

Yes, you can include chocolate chips in molded cookies—in a layer.

 1 cup (225 grams) unsalted butter
 1 large egg
 ½ cup (120 milliliters) agave syrup (or other syrup)
 1 tablespoon cream
 1 teaspoon vanilla
 ½ cup (100 grams) dark brown sugar
 ¼ teaspoon salt
 About 4½ cups (630 grams) all-purpose flour (plain
    flour)
 About ¼ cup very finely chopped walnuts
 About ¼ cup mini chocolate chips or chopped chocolate
    chips

1. Melt the butter and set aside.

2. Beat the egg in a large bowl until yolk and white are fully mixed.

3. Mix the honey, cream, and brandy flavoring. Add to the egg and beat until well mixed.

4. Mix the brown sugar, cinnamon, cloves, mace, cardamom and salt. Add to the egg mixture and beat until well mixed.

5. Add the melted butter slowly and beat until well mixed.

6. Add flour until the mixture is solid enough to knead.

7. Transfer to your work surface and knead in more all-purpose flour (plain flour) to make a soft, slightly sticky dough.

8. Divide the dough into two pieces, one about twice the size of the other.

9. Put the smaller piece aside.

10. Knead the nuts and chocolate chips into the larger piece

11. Follow directions for making layer cookies, found in the January section of this book.

12. Chill the cookies while you preheat the oven to 350°F (177°C).

13. Bake for 10 to 15 minutes or until slightly browned at the edges.

Recipe: Orange Cookies

These are great with the chocolate backing I describe in the January section. Also great by themselves.

1 cup (225 grams) unsalted butter
1 large egg
½ cup (120 milliliters) honey
1 tablespoon freshly squeezed orange juice
1 teaspoon freshly squeezed lemon juice
1 teaspoon natural orange flavoring
⅛ teaspoon natural orange oil
½ cup (100 grams) sugar
2 teaspoons finely grated orange peel
1 teaspoon finely grated lemon peel
⅛ teaspoon salt
About 4½ cups (630 grams) all-purpose flour (plain flour)

1. Melt the butter and set aside.

2. Beat the egg in a large bowl until the yolk and white are fully mixed.

3. Mix the honey, orange juice, lemon juice, orange flavoring, and orange oil. Add to the egg and beat until well mixed.

4. Mix the sugar, orange peel, lemon peel, and salt. Add to the egg mixture and beat until well mixed. If the mixture isn't smooth, don't worry—it will become smooth as you add the flour.

5. Add the melted butter slowly and beat until well mixed. Don't just pour it in quickly—the heat still in the butter could cook the egg!

6. Add flour slowly and mix in until you have dough that is solid enough to knead.

7. Transfer the dough to a floured work surface. Continue adding flour by kneading in a little at a time until the dough is smooth and slightly sticky.

8. Wrap or cover the dough to prevent drying, then refrigerate to make it less sticky. This should take half an hour at most.

9. Roll and form the dough.

10. Refrigerate the cookies while you preheat the oven to 350°F (175°C).

11. Bake for 10 to 15 minutes or until the edges have slightly browned and the top has begun to firm up.

NOVEMBER

Late Fall—An Appreciation

Fall is one of my favorite times of year. The sudden change in sunlight, from clear to golden, a new scent in the wind, a new school year. Fall has always seemed to me to be a season of beginnings, not endings.

Here on San Juan Island, fall is everywhere. Leaves turn to yellow, brown, and orange, swirl from hill to hill. Garden tools retreat from the aisles of the hardware store, replaced by fireplace logs and road salt. Old pear orchards, untended for years, bear heavily among tall weeds. The pears are harvested only by deer and raccoons. Pumpkins are piled outside the market, and the new crop of apples dazzles us.

And the windstorms begin. I'm told I live on the windy side of the island, and I believe it. Some November nights, the southwest wind sounds like a freight train. I grew up in hurricane country, and I've never heard winds quite like this.

Surprisingly, though, there has never been any damage—aside from losing the seat cushion from a lawn chair when we first moved here. We looked and looked, but never found it. I imagine that seat cushion sailing through the night air like a Frisbee, maybe sailing out to sea. Neptune may be sitting on it this minute, for all I know. We're wiser now—when wind is in the forecast, we bring the chairs in.

Here at the 49th parallel, fall is over by the end of November. Winter doesn't start officially until the solstice, December 21, but the year itself knows no such rule. Late November in the islands is cold. We close our windows at night now, and our footsteps crackle on frost in the early morning. Often, we have snow around Thanksgiving. It's a good time to celebrate houses, brightly lit and welcoming—our own, or our friends'—a good time to be home, or to entertain. The scent of baking cookies fills the kitchen. We hear the storms outside and count our blessings.

It's time to pause and feel thankful for all we have. And many cultures do this at harvest time, whenever it occurs. Traditional harvest celebrations include Sukkot, Harvest Home, Festival of the Autumn Moon, Martinmas, Thanksgiving, and many more.

This month, let's look at cookies to celebrate the earth's bounty. November's recipes feature the flavors I associate with autumn— nuts, cranberries, apples, pumpkin, and warm spices.

Recipe: Apple or Pumpkin Cookie Tartlets

These require a special mold—usually called a "pineapple tart mold." It's intended for an Indonesian specialty, but these molds make wonderful cookies as well, and are very easy to use.

1 cup (225 grams) butter

1 large egg

½ cup (120 milliliters) apple jelly or honey (I like apple jelly for apple tartlets and honey for the pumpkin tartlets.)

1 teaspoon vanilla extract

1 tablespoon milk

½ cup or 100 grams sugar

¼ teaspoon salt

About 4 cups (585 grams) all-purpose flour (plain flour)

1. Melt the butter. Set aside.

2. Beat the egg in a large bowl.

3. Mix the honey or jelly, vanilla extract, and milk. Add to the egg.

4. Mix the sugar and salt. Add to the egg mixture.

5. Add the butter slowly to the egg mixture and beat well.

6. Add flour slowly until the mixture is solid enough to knead. If you are using an electric mixer, stop the mixer once or twice as you add flour, and scrape the sides of the bowl to get all the flour mixed in.

7. Transfer the dough to a counter or breadboard and knead in more flour to make a soft, slightly sticky dough.

8. Wrap and refrigerate the dough for 30 minutes.

9. Roll and form the dough.

10. Chill the cookies while you preheat the oven to 350°F (177°C).

11. Bake for 10 to 15 minutes or until slightly browned at the edges.

12. Fill with commercial pumpkin pie or apple pie filling, pumpkin or apple butter, or with your own pre-cooked pumpkin or apple pie filling. It's best to add the filling just before serving.

Recipe: Cinnamon Chestnut Cookies

These cookies are crisp, on account of the high proportion of nuts. Make them thin for best results.

> 1 cup (225 grams) butter
> 1 large egg
> ½ cup (160 grams) sweetened chestnut paste
> 1 teaspoon vanilla extract
> 1 tablespoon cream
> ½ cup (100 grams) sugar
> ⅛ teaspoon salt
> 1 teaspoon cinnamon
> About 1¼ (165 grams) all-purpose flour (plain flour)

1. Tear the chestnut paste into marble sized bits.
2. Melt the butter.
3. Combine the warm butter and the chestnut paste and beat well until smooth.
4. Beat together the egg, vanilla extract, and cream and add to the butter mixture.
5. Combine the sugar, salt, and cinnamon, and add to the butter mixture

6. Add flour slowly until the mixture is solid enough to knead

7. Transfer to a work surface and knead in more flour to make a dough the consistency of children's modeling clay.

8. Roll and form the dough.

9. Preheat the oven to 350°F (175°C).

10. Bake one test cookie for about 15 minutes. Adjust time and temperature as needed, and bake the remainder of the cookies.

Recipe: Cranberry Pecan Layer Cookies

Use a mold that will look good with a tweedy, flecked cookie.

> 1 cup (225 grams) butter
> 1 large egg
> ½ cup (120 milliliters) honey
> ½ cup (100 grams) sugar
> ½ cup (80 grams) finely ground pecans
> ¼ teaspoon salt
> About 3¾cups (515 grams) all-purpose flour (plain flour)
> 1 cup (170 grams) finely chopped dried cranberries

1. Melt the butter. Set aside.

2. Beat the egg in a large bowl.

3. Add the honey to the egg mixture.

4. Mix the sugar, ground nuts, and salt. Add to the egg mixture.

5. Add the butter slowly and beat well.

6. Add flour slowly until the mixture is solid enough to knead. If you are using an electric mixer, stop the mixer once or twice as you add flour, and scrape the sides of the bowl to get all the flour mixed in.

7. Follow the instructions in the January section to make the layers.

8. Chill the cookies while you preheat the oven to 350°F (177°C).

9. Bake for 10 to 15 minutes or until slightly browned at the edges.

Tip: Butter Molds for Cookies

"Can you use a butter mold to make molded cookies?"

I sometimes get asked that. It's one of those questions that gets a roundabout answer. Basically, it depends on the butter mold.

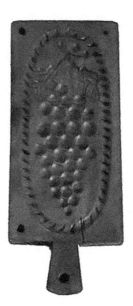

Shown is the one I use for cookies. As you can see, it's a flat plate. It does have another piece, a jointed top section that fits over this part. The top section forms the sides of the butter pat—it's like a little fence. I haven't made molded butter, but I suppose butter is molded soft and the mold is removed when the butter is hardened. The molding piece would then be pried off.

The holes you see in this mold are used to fasten the top piece onto it with removable dowels. I have the top piece, and it's certainly interesting, though not of any use in cookie molding. Generally, any mold you find that shows holes like this is intended for something besides cookies—sometimes butter, sometimes chocolate or marzipan.

But many of them work well for cookies. The multi-part mold is likely to, especially if the part that forms the design is shallow, as this one is.

Molds that are deeper than the thickness of a cookie should be avoided. There just is no good way to get the cookie out. So if your shaped piece is more than about a quarter of an inch deep, and the sides don't come off, I wouldn't recommend it.

You may notice that this mold is cracked. This makes no difference when you're using honey cookie recipes such as mine, because you don't have to tap or strike the mold to release the cookie. Honey recipes are also good for porcelain cookie molds, or other fragile molds.

Very tender shortbread dough often molds better in butter molds than in many cookie molds.

DECEMBER

December Holidays

It's cold now, here on San Juan Island. Snow is a possibility every morning, and frost is a certainty. The trees are bare, but we bundle up in layer upon layer of coats and sweaters.

And the days are so short. The sun comes up, far in the south, long after breakfast, and it sets long before dinner. This is the time of year when many cultures have celebrations to drive away the dark—Christmas, with all its lights and its star; Hanukkah, the festival of lights; Kwanzaa; Santa Lucia; midwinter festivals in several cultures; and many others throughout history.

Many homeowners on the island put up Christmas lights, of course, doubly welcome outside the town limits, where there are no streetlights.

There are decorations, too. I have a tiny model village I put on the mantel for Christmas, and it usually stays for most of the winter. The merchants of Friday Harbor help drive away the dark with a competition to decorate their shop fronts.

On December 5, we celebrate St. Nicholas Eve with molded cookies in the shape of the saint with his horse or donkey—some cookie molds show one, some the other. The story of St. Nicholas is not well-known, but he was a real person who performed great acts of generosity and kindness.

It was St. Nicholas cookies that originally sparked my own interest in molded cookies. My husband, Aaron Shepard, is a children's author, and his children's storybook *The Baker's Dozen* is about a baker who learns a lesson of generosity from St. Nicholas himself.

Near the end of December is the winter solstice, that turning point that tells us that the sun is coming back, even as we see only cold and darkness.

The month ends, of course, with its cornucopia of Christmas cookies! These include almost every secular and religious motif you could think of, from jolly snowmen to medieval manger scenes. Baking cookies for family and friends is a special holiday joy, and in the spirit of St. Nicholas, let's bake some to give away as well.

For this month, I feature both traditional and new recipes to bake and share.

Recipe: Cinnamon Almond Treats

Use this recipe to make a molded cookie version of Cinnamon Stars, or make it into cookie tartlets with a raspberry filling for Cookie Linzer Torte. You'll find detailed directions for cookie tartlets at the beginning of this book.

These cookies have a texture somewhat similar to macaroons—soft and slightly sticky. Be careful not to overbake them.

    ¾ cup (235 grams) almond paste
    ½ cup (115 grams) unsalted butter
    1 large egg
    ½ cup (120 milliliters) honey
    ¼ cup (60 milliliters) cream
    ½ teaspoon almond extract
    ½ teaspoon natural lemon flavoring
    ½ cup (100 grams) sugar
    2 teaspoons ground cinnamon
    ½ teaspoon salt
    About 4 cups (560 grams) all-purpose flour (plain flour)

1. Chop the almond paste, or tear into bits about the size of a small grape.

2. Combine the almond paste and butter in a heatproof container. Warm in a low oven or microwave until the butter is melted. Beat well on high speed until smooth.

3. Add the egg and beat until well mixed.

4. Mix the honey, milk, almond extract, and lemon flavoring. Add to the butter mixture and beat until well mixed.

5. Mix the sugar, cinnamon, and salt. Add to the butter mixture and beat until well mixed.

6. Add flour slowly until the mixture is solid enough to knead.

7. Transfer to your work surface and knead in more flour to make a soft, slightly sticky dough.

8. Wrap or cover the dough and refrigerate for up to 30 minutes, until it is firm but still flexible.

9. Roll and form the dough.

10. Bake for 10 to 15 minutes or until the edges have slightly browned and the top has begun to firm up. Be careful to avoid overbaking, or the cookies will become too hard as they cool.

Notes

For an extra-special dessert cookie, apply chocolate backing (see the January section), using white chocolate flavored with a little cinnamon and/or finely grated lemon peel.

For the Cookie Linzer Torte filling, use seedless raspberry jam, which you may mix with soft cream cheese or almond paste. If desired, flavor to taste with cinnamon, finely grated lemon peel, and/or raspberry liqueur.

Recipe: Honey Cream Cookies

Any kind of honey is good, but this cookie is especially nice if you use strong-flavored honey such as sage or maple. You can add flavoring extracts if you want lemon, orange, almond, or whatever.

This recipe makes a soft, mild-flavored cookie. Because it's sweetened with 100% honey, it works especially well with large molds such as House on the Hill's Shepherd Nativity, shown here.

The cookie is shown packaged for giving, using a cake board and shrink-wrap. You could add ribbons or other trim to complete your package.

½ cup (115 grams) butter
½ cup (120 grams) softened cream cheese
1 large egg
¼ teaspoon salt
1 cup (240 milliliters) honey
1 teaspoon vanilla extract
2 tablespoons whipping cream
About 4 cups (550 grams) all-purpose flour (plain flour)

1. Melt the butter. Add the cream cheese, broken into small pieces. Set aside.

2. Beat the egg in a large bowl. Add the salt and mix well.

3. Mix the honey, vanilla extract, and cream. Add to the egg.

4. Add the butter mixture slowly to the egg mixture and beat well.

5. Add flour slowly until the mixture is solid enough to knead. If you're using an electric mixer, stop the mixer once or twice as you're adding flour, and scrape the sides of the bowl to get all the flour mixed in.

6. Transfer the dough to your work surface and knead in more flour to make a soft, slightly sticky dough.

7. Wrap and refrigerate the dough for 30 minutes.

8. Roll and form the dough.

9. Chill the cookies while you preheat the oven to 350°F (177°C).

10. Bake small cookies for 10 to 15 minutes until slightly browned at the edges. If you're making a very large cookie such as the Shepherd Nativity, which is ten inches in diameter, use a lower the oven temperature—300°F (150°C). Bake until firm. This will probably be much longer than the time given for smaller cookies, so check the cookie about every ten minutes.

Notes

Since the dough is very pale, make sure it's perfectly smooth before you mold the cookie—otherwise, any wrinkles will show up and spoil the design. If you want a stronger flavor, 1-2 teaspoons of flavoring extract may be added. Almond, rum, or brandy extract would be good choices.

Tip: Good Prints from Extra-Large Molds

Large molds can present a special problem—you may not get a good print across the whole mold unless you work carefully.

Most large cookies, for instance, have beautiful, ornate borders. This is the area where I have had the most trouble. Make sure to press hard all around the border, or you'll have an incomplete print.

Watch out for other "special points" on the mold as well. In the Shepherd Nativity mold, which I used for the cookie in the preceding recipe, the special points are the baby in the manger, the people's faces, and the animal heads. If you get an incomplete print on any of these, the cookie won't look good.

I had a lot of trouble with this until I marked the back of the cookie mold with a permanent marker, putting an X behind each point that needed special attention. I actually pound on the mold with my fist at those points to make sure I get a good print.

For more tips, see the discussion of this particular mold in the basic directions at the beginning of this book.

Tip: Handling Oversize Cookies

Oversize cookies are delicate, especially when they're hot. And most spatulas and cookie lifters are too small to be useful with cookies a foot or more in height.

Of course, you make oversize cookies on a sheet of foil or parchment, and that's helpful in handling them. But, especially for the very large "exhibition cookies," a foot or more tall, a flexible sheet may not work well by itself.

Fortunately, there are several great tools to help with this, but they aren't cookie utensils. You'll find the best tools for oversize cookies if you look for pizza and barbecue utensils.

You can sometimes find barbecue spatulas big enough to flip a whole steak on a grill. And pizza lifters come in different sizes, from about twelve inches round to the huge "peel" that's used for large pizzas.

Even a cookie sheet can be used as a lifter, if it has one or more flat edges. Just don't try to move a large cookie that's right out of the oven without supporting the entire thing.

The cookies are easier to handle when they've cooled thoroughly, but of course, you have to move them to get them onto a cooling rack.

Recipe: Maple Gingerbread Cookies

1 cup (225 grams) unsalted butter

1 large egg

2 tablespoons brown sugar or maple sugar

6 tablespoons granulated sugar

1 teaspoon cinnamon

½ teaspoon ground ginger

¼ teaspoon salt

½ cup (120 milliliters) maple syrup (See note.)

1 tablespoon finely grated fresh ginger, optional (See note.)

About 4 cups (574 grams) all-purpose flour (plain flour)

1. Melt the butter and set aside.

2. Beat the egg in a large bowl until the yolk and white are fully mixed.

3. Mix the sugar, brown or maple sugar, ground ginger, cinnamon, and salt. Sift this mixture to remove lumps.

4. Add the sugar mixture to the egg.

5. Mix the maple syrup and grated ginger and add to the egg mixture.

6. Add the butter slowly and beat well.

7. Add flour slowly until the mixture is solid enough to knead.

8. Transfer to a counter or breadboard and knead in more flour to make a soft, slightly sticky dough.

9. Wrap or cover the dough and refrigerate for up to 30 minutes, until it is firm but still flexible.

10. Roll and form the dough with a cavity mold according to directions in the January section of this book.

11. Chill the cookies while you preheat the oven to 350°F or 175° C.

12. Bake about 15 minutes or until slightly browned at the edges.

Notes

I used to look for Grade B maple syrup for baking, but the grade names have changed recently. For the strong flavor that used to be desirable in maple baked goods, look for "Grade A: Dark Color & Robust Flavor."

Here's how to get super-fine grated ginger: When you buy the ginger root, wash it and freeze it, peel and all. Never let this ginger thaw. You can't re-freeze it.

Grate it frozen. I use a Microplane grater (and the protective glove made for it—those things can really slice your hands). I lay the ginger on a cutting board and rub the grater over it—I find it faster and easier than rubbing the ginger on the grater.

If you don't want the extra-spicy taste of fresh ginger, you can use 1 tablespoon of powdered ginger instead. If you do, add it to the sugar mixture along with the cinnamon.

Recipe: Chocolate Raspberry Cookie Tartlets

More cookie tartlets! I chose the tart mold for these because the dark chocolate dough is too dark for most molds. If you need directions for using the tart molds, you'll find them at the beginning of this book.

4 ounces (115 grams) bittersweet or dark chocolate
½ cup (115 grams) unsalted butter
1 large egg
½ cup (100 grams) sugar
½ teaspoon salt
2 tablespoons baking cocoa
2 tablespoons raspberry liqueur (See note.)
1 teaspoon vanilla extract
1 teaspoon chocolate extract
About 2 cups (280 grams) all-purpose flour (plain flour)

1. Warm the chocolate and butter together in a low oven or microwave until the chocolate is soft and the butter is melted. The chocolate may hold its shape when soft, so test with a spoon to avoid overcooking.

2. Stir the chocolate and butter together. Set aside.

3. Beat the egg in a large bowl until yolk and white are fully mixed.

4. Mix the sugar, salt, and cocoa. Sift to remove lumps.

5. Add the sugar mixture to the egg.

6. Add the liqueur, vanilla extract, and chocolate extract to the egg mixture.

7. Add the chocolate mixture to the egg mixture.

8. Add flour slowly until the dough is solid enough to knead.

9. Knead in additional flour until the dough is the consistency of children's modeling clay.

10. Using a tart mold, press out cookie tart shells. Complete illustrated directions for using cookie tart shells are located at the beginning of this book.

11. Bake the cookies at 350°F (175°C) for ten to twelve minutes.

Notes

For the raspberry liqueur, you may substitute 2 teaspoons raspberry flavoring.

For the raspberry filling, you may use sieved raspberry jam. Or mix it with softened cream cheese, and/or raspberry liqueur.

If you prefer, substitute other flavorings or liqueur such as hazelnut, coffee, or almond for the raspberry liqueur, and fill the tart shells with chocolate buttercream, chocolate almond butter, Nutella, or other filling of your choice.

Recipe: Pecan Cookies

Pecans are a special Christmas treat, and they make wonderful cookies. The toasted flavor that develops as they bake is really delicious. For this recipe, use a mold design that will look good with a slightly tweedy, flecked appearance.

    1 cup (225 grams) butter
    1 large egg
    ½ cup (120 milliliters) honey
    ½ cup (98 grams) brown sugar
    ½ cup (80 grams) finely ground pecans, see note
    ¼ teaspoon salt
    About 4¼ cups (560 grams) all-purpose flour (plain
        flour)

1. Melt the butter. Set aside.

2. Beat the egg in a large bowl.

3. Add the honey to the egg mixture.

4. Mix the brown sugar, ground nuts, and salt. Add to the egg mixture.

5. Add the butter slowly and beat well.

6. Add flour slowly until the mixture is solid enough to knead. If you're using an electric mixer, stop the mixer once or twice as you're adding flour, and scrape the sides of the bowl to get all the flour mixed in.

7. Transfer to a counter or breadboard and knead in a little more flour if required to make a soft, slightly sticky dough.

8. Wrap and refrigerate the dough for 30 minutes.

9. Roll and form the dough.

10. Chill the cookies while you preheat the oven to 350°F (177°C).

11. Bake for 10-15 minutes or until slightly browned at the edges.

Notes

You may be able to buy ground nuts, or you can grind them in a food processor or blender with a cup or two of the flour (which keeps the nuts from turning into nut butter).

Tip: More on Trimming Cookies

If your cookie has enclosed areas that aren't part of the design, you have a choice—to trim them out or not. They can be attractive either way. Shown here is a St. Nicholas cookie from the same mold as in the recipe above, but this time untrimmed.

If you do trim around the horse's legs and bridle, and the Saint's arm and staff, there are a few tricks to make it easier.

1. Chill the cookie well before doing any trimming, either the outline or the details. Leave as much dough as possible around the edge.

2. Use a sharp craft knife.

3. Trim out the details before trimming around the edges of the cookie. The cookie is much less likely to tear if you trim the small, delicate pieces first.

Tip: Christmas Ornaments from Molded Cookies

There are two ways to do this. One is to make real cookies and use them as ornaments, as in this photo of a cookie from a mold by Gene Wilson of HOBI Cookie Molds. This is feasible if you live in a climate where bugs and other pests aren't a problem.

You'll need to select forms that can be secured to the tree, or you can wrap the cookies tightly in plastic wrap or shrink-wrap and secure the wrap to the tree. In the photo, if you look closely, you can see a loop of clear fishing line around the angel's waist.

If you use real cookies, you'll probably throw them away at the end of the season, or you could pack them carefully in freezer containers and freeze them for re-use the next year—however, I've only done this with plain cookies, and don't know whether it would work if they're frosted.

Another way to have molded cookie ornaments is to use polymer clay, salt clay, or papier-mâché in your cookie molds. However, I doubt if this is a good idea with a mold that shouldn't be washed, such as a wood mold. Not if you're planning to use it for food again.

Whatever medium you use, follow the directions that come with the art material.

For paper or clay cookies, you can embed thin wire in the backs for fasteners. Or glue the wire to the cookie, using a glue recommended by the manufacturer of the art material. You'll get a better bond if you thread your wire through a piece of cloth and glue that to the back of the cookie. The cloth should cover as much as possible of the cookie without showing from the front, because the larger the glue contact area, the better the bond.

For outdoor ornaments such as wreaths, art materials would be the only practical choice. You can make a wreath entirely out of different-colored cookies "decorated" with acrylic paints, or you can attach clay or paper cookies to a natural or artificial wreath.

More Credits

Mold makers are cited in the text for nearly all the contemporary molds and for some of the cookies made from them. Here are additional credits for mold makers, listed by section and article to help you find the molds.

Front Pages

Spring ~ HOBI Cookie Molds (Easter Bunny), House on the Hill (Thistle and Rose), Brown Bag Cookie Molds (Wheelbarrow)

Summer ~ House on the Hill (Springerle rolling pin), Brown Bag Cookie Molds (Wedding Heart), My Cookie Mold (Sun)

Autumn ~ Brown Bag Cookie Molds (Fraidy Cat), Pampered Chef (Ohio Star Heart), House on the Hill (Harvest)

Winter ~ HOBI Cookie Molds (Saint Nicholas), House on the Hill (Crown)

Title page ~ Pampered Chef

January

First Story: Journey to the Twelfth-Night Market ~ Jan VandeVoorde

Recipe: Spiced Lemon Pecan "King" Cookies ~ House on the Hill

Recipe: Raisin Layer Cookies ~ The Springerle Baker

Recipe: Spice Cookies ~ My Cookie Mold

Third Story: The White Cat ~ HOBI Cookie Molds

Recipe: Chocolate Coconut Tea Cookies ~ House on the Hill

Recipe: Lime Cookies ~ Brown Bag Cookie Molds

February

Recipe: Dark Chocolate Cookies with Marzipan Topping ~ House on the Hill

Tip: Working with Marzipan ~ Springerle Joy

Tip: Trimming Cookies ~ Hartstone

Recipe: I-Love-You Cookies ~ Brown Bag Cookie Molds

Recipe: Chocolate Orange Layer Cookies ~ HOBI Cookie Molds

Recipe: Sweets-for-the-Sweet Sugar Cookies ~ Springerle Joy

March

Tip: Creating Your Own Shortbread Recipes ~ House on the Hill

Shortbread Pans ~ Zanda Panda

Recipe: Tropical Shortbread ~ House on the Hill (Springerle rolling pin)

Tip: The Perfect Traditional Shortbread ~ S. R. White Carving

April

Recipe: Coconut Sugar Cookies ~ Brown Bag Cookie Molds

Recipe: Cherry and Chocolate Layer Cookies ~ HOBI Cookie Molds

Tip: Honey and Sugar—Getting the Right Proportions ~ House on the Hill

Recipe: Chocolate Sugar Cookies ~ HOBI Cookie Molds

Recipe: Pecan Cookies with Chocolate Backing ~ My Cookie Mold

May

Recipe: Soft Brandy Orange Cookies ~ Brown Bag Cookie Molds

Twentieth-Century Pottery Cookie Molds ~ Brown Bag Cookie Molds

Recipe: Cinnamon Almond Cookies ~ Brown Bag Cookie Molds

June

Recipe: Easy Wedding Cookies ~ Springerle Joy

Wedding Cookie Molds ~ The Springerle Baker (Wedding Coach), House on the Hill (Bridal Arch)

November

Recipe: Cinnamon Chestnut Cookies ~ House on the Hill

December

December Holidays ~ HOBI Cookie Molds

Recipe: Cinnamon Almond Treats ~ House on the Hill

Recipe: Maple Gingerbread Cookies ~ HOBI Cookie Molds

Back Pages

About the Author ~ Brown Bag Cookie Molds

All tart molds are from Brown Cookie.

ANNE L. WATSON is the author of *Baking with Cookie Molds* and a number of other popular books on home crafts and lifestyle, as well as children's books and many novels. In a previous career, she was a historic preservation architecture consultant. Anne and her husband, Aaron Shepard, now live in Bellingham, Washington. You can visit her online and ask her questions at

www.annelwatson.com

Also for cookie mold lovers . . .

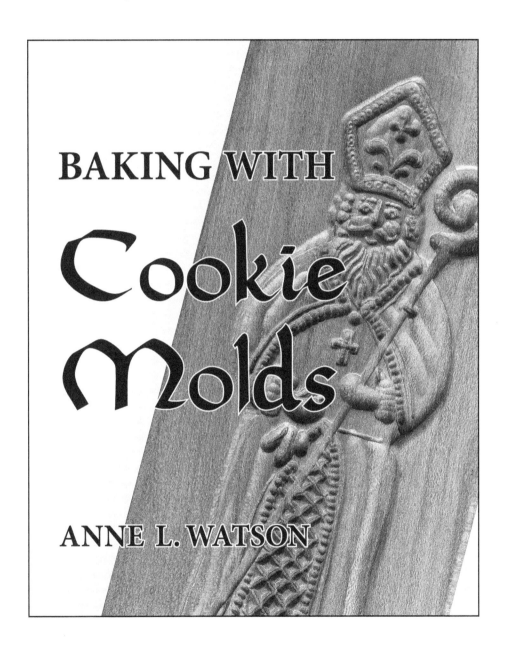

BAKING WITH

Cookie

Molds

ANNE L. WATSON

Books by Anne

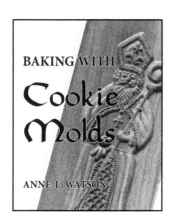

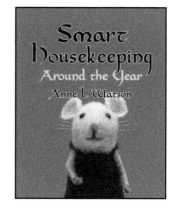

Books by Anne

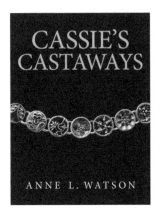

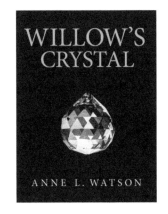

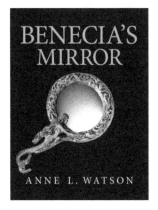

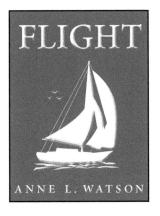

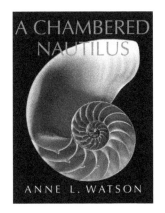

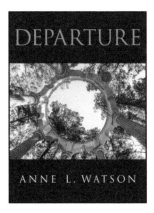

Books by Anne